Praise for

A Guide to Governing Charities

In this wonderful guide to board governance, Ted Hull offers the leaders of charities and the boards that govern, them helpful and clear insight on the issues they face in today's world. Using an easy-to-read narrative format, and responding to questions that leaders and directors ask when dealing with governance issues, he addresses issues with clarity and simplicity.

Readers of *A Guide to Governing Charities* will find greater effectiveness and increased efficiency as they better understand their roles in the work as leaders and directors of charities in Canada. This book will be of great value to those who wish to better understand their role in helping charities move toward a shared goal and purpose—from where they are to where they want to be.

DR. RILEY COULTER
Chair, Siloam Mission; Winnipeg
Chancellor, Ambrose University College; Calgary

Where was this book when I was beginning to learn this stuff? Ted Hull has given a gift to leaders, pastors, board members, committee people—anyone involved in leading or guiding a group or an organization. This gift is clear, it's instructive, it's delightful, and most important it is helpful. It is the gift of wisdom. If you want to learn how to lead an organization, or do a better job of leading your organization, *A Guide to Governing Charities* is a book you must read.

JAMEY MCDONALD
Executive Director, Baptist General Conference of Canada

Ted Hull has given the Charity community a great service with this book. Navigating the relational, legal, and practical elements of being in Charity leadership can be an overwhelming challenge – particularly when many of these leaders serve as volunteers who have plenty of other responsibilities in life. Ted has been able to take these challenges and make the solutions easy to understand and implement. The people that charities have been built to serve deserve the very best organization and leadership in order to ensure viability, sustainability, and effectiveness. This book is an important guide to assist Charity leaders toward that goal.

KIRK GILES
President, Promise Keepers Canada

A Guide to Governing Charities is not the first book on *Policy Governance®* that I've read, nor will it be the last. But it's the most readable. Ted writes as keenly and insightfully as he speaks in person, and here he condenses his expertise for those Board Members and Leaders who desire to be more effective. Ted sharpens me every time I'm around him, and here he does it again!

BILL EHLERS
Canadian Board Chair and Member of the International Board, Avant Ministries, International

A wise grandfather was known to ask his grandson each day as the boy walked home from school. "So - did you ask any good questions today?" Building each chapter around a question that board members often ask (or ought to ask), the book provides well researched, no nonsense answers in an engaging and entertaining style. Much like a conversation with its author, this book provides good answers in clear language. If you can't ask these questions to Ted personally, working your way through *A Guide to Governing Charities* is the next best thing.

TOM CASTOR
Senior Pastor, Grant Memorial Church

Ted Hull lives and breathes efficient systems and methods of organization. In this book, he shares his expertise, in a clear, concise and logical fashion. From dream to inception to operations, this book lays out the steps to take and the pitfalls to avoid when creating or restructuring a Charity and its governing Board. Ted's conversational style of writing ensures that potentially heavy subject matter is delivered in a relaxed, easy-to-read book, packed with gems of wisdom. This book is destined to be mandatory reading for Charity leadership teams across Canada.

RON PEARCE
Executive Director/Founder, Empower Ministries

Ted is passionate about organizations governing themselves in an orderly, efficient and excellent manner. *A Guide to Governing Charities* makes an important contribution by raising awareness of the importance of excellence in organizational governance; to recognize that good stewardship demands good governance practices and procedures. Ted also stresses the importance of organizations achieving and maintaining compliance with all applicable legal requirements, which in my experience, can be easily overlooked by organizations as they understandably focus on carrying out their mission statements in their day-to-day operations.

Ted addresses the most common issues that organizations confront, and in doing so offers a "plain language" explanation of important governance concepts, combined with practical advice that readers will find helpful.

NORMAN R. PIEL
Lawyer

A Guide to
GOVERNING
CHARITIES

Success in the Boardroom
Starts with Asking the Right Questions

Ted Hull

A GUIDE TO GOVERNING CHARITIES

Copyright © 2011 by Ted Hull

Policy Governance® is a registered service mark of John Carver.

ISBN: 978-1-77069-371-5

Printed in Canada.

Word Alive Press
131 Cordite Road, Winnipeg, MB R3W 1S1
www.wordalivepress.ca

WORD ALIVE PRESS
Just Write!

Library and Archives Canada Cataloguing in Publication

Hull, Ted, 1951-

    A guide to governing charities / Ted Hull.

ISBN 978-1-77069-371-5

    1. Charities--Management--Miscellanea. 2. Strategic planning--Miscellanea. 3. Boards of directors--Miscellanea.

    I. Title.

HD62.6.H83 2011   658.4'012   C2011-905539-2

To Dad

Your first glimpse of the Saviour was the Answer;
rendering every earthly question irrelevant.

Table of Contents

Acknowledgements

Thank you, Karin, for your gracious editing of this book. I am grateful my readers will never know what the first draft looked like.

Thank you to everyone at Word Alive Press. You had such patience in putting the pieces of this project together after I dumped them on your desk.

Thank you, Marcie, for reading my first draft… and telling me it was actually interesting… in a way that only a daughter could do.

Thank you, Brian, for inspiring me to follow through on this project by authoring your own book. Dads need sons to look up to.

Thank you, Alyssa, for praying and asking God to "help Grandpa finish the book and get it published." I didn't realize ten-year-olds knew that books needed to be published.

Thank you, Lorna, that when you asked what I was doing, you graciously accepted the same answer time after time: "The book."

Thank you, Lord, for inspiring, empowering and energizing me to do what I would not even have had an interest in doing myself.

Introduction

The Chairman called to ask for my input on the agenda for an upcoming Board meeting. I pointed out that some governance issues should be dealt with, including the Board completing its annual self-evaluation. "Can we postpone the governance stuff to the following meeting?" he asked. "Our Board is not really interested in governance."

"You have *got* to be kidding," I muttered to myself. (I didn't express that to him because he was a client after all.)

I'm a doctor but I can't stand the sight of blood. I love teaching; it's the students I can't stand. Racing cars would be great if it wasn't for the speed. I'm in love with life, but this breathing thing is a hassle. I like sitting on a Board, I'm just not into this governance thing.

It was that response that led in part to the writing of this book.

Governance is the only real reason for a Board's existence. Boards don't (or shouldn't) exist to help the Leader run the organization, offer opinions, have a handle on all the details, tweak the budget, control the administration or advance a personal agenda.

So then, what is governance? What *is* a Board supposed to do? This book is about asking the right questions as you approach issues of governance and the management of a Charity and then providing you with some high-level answers to point you in the direction of more detailed answers.

This book is not intended to be the definitive answer, the authoritative work or the final word on governance. However, through this book I want to provide you with a great helicopter ride and point out some of the sites that you should note. We won't get close enough to see all the details, but hopefully by the end of the book you will have a good perspective of the charities landscape. There will be some readers who have already toured the sites and will want to point out some attractions I have not mentioned. Okay, *attractions* when it comes to governance might seem like an oxymoron, but you get my point. The challenge with too much detail is that by the time we fly low over every monument, some passengers will have run out of energy and our helicopter will have run out of fuel.

Turtle on a Fencepost

Individuals, usually in reference to politicians, have used the post turtle analogy. When you seen a turtle on a fencepost you know (a) it didn't get up there by itself; (b) it doesn't belong there; (c) it can't get anything done while it's there; and (d) you just want to help the dumb thing down. While I trust my time on the fencepost is not a waste of my time or yours, I will readily acknowledge that I haven't gotten here by myself. I am on the governance fencepost because many individuals have unwittingly helped me get there. These include mentors, employers, peers and clients.

There are also great authors whose books on governance have influenced me and which I can confidently recommend. *Boards That Make a Difference*[i] and *Reinventing Your Board*[ii] by John Carver, the creator of the Policy Governance® model are two foundational books. *Getting Started with Policy Governance*[iii] by Caroline Oliver is an easy-to-read handbook on how to implement Policy Governance. *The Charities Handbook,*[iv] published by the Canadian Council of Christian Charities, ought to be at the fingertips of anyone involved in a leadership role within a Canadian Charity. Jim Brown does a great job of illustrating the role of Boards in telling a story of typical Board work in his book, *The Imperfect Board Member.*[v] You can familiarize yourself with some of the legal issues as they relate to governance by reading Dick Kranendonk's book, *Serving As a Board Member.*[vi] If your focus is Church governance, you must read *Elders and Leaders,*[vii] a carefully thought through book by Gene Getz. Finally, in my mind, Aubrey Malphurs[viii] has been so helpful to the charities community in his clear and straightforward approach to leadership.

In the governance field there are various terms used to describe the same or similar things. For the purpose of clarity, I want to be consistent in using the same word to describe the same thing. Terms such as *organization*, *not-for-profit*, NGO (non-government organization), *mission*, *para-church* or *church* are used to describe what I will be talking about. As you read this book, one or more of those terms may fit your context. However, the term I will typically use is *Charity*. Near the end of the book I have devoted a chapter to talking specifically about the unique challenges of church leadership.

The head of the organization you have in mind may be referred to as the executive director, president, CEO, lead pastor, senior pastor, head minister, grand poo-bah or her highness or even other less complimentary terms… but I digress. The term I will use is *Leader*. I realize not many charities formally refer to the head of their organization as the *Leader*, but it's the word I will use for this book.

Each Charity has legal owners. The term I will use to describe those individuals is *Members*.

There can be confusion between the *Members* as legal owners and those people who sit on a Board who are commonly referred to as board members. To minimize the confusion, board members will be referred to as *Directors*.

The positions of directors and leaders within the charities community are still typically occupied by males. The tendency therefore is to refer to an individual Director or Leader by using the masculine pronoun *he* or *him* and the possessive pronoun *his*. It is my view that to do so will continue to stereotype the Director and Leader roles as being designed for men. An option for addressing this dilemma would be to use the more accurate but awkward pronouns, *he/she*, *him/her* and *his/hers*.

Jila Ghomeshi in her book *Grammar Matters*[ix] asks, "What if you want to refer to a single individual whose gender you do not know? … For instance what if someone says 'I saw the strangest person on the bus today…' and you want to ask about that person?" She points out that "Prescriptive grammarians have traditionally recommended the use of *he* as a generic over *he or she*, which has been declared 'clumsy.' Ordinary people on the other hand, have been quite comfortable using the word *they (as in* 'why were they strange'?)"[1] (Ghomeshi 31) Assuming that I am writing to ordinary people, I will use the term *they* rather than the more clumsy *he or she*.

So many charities are diligent and persevere at doing great work, but they are encumbered and hindered by organizational structures that slow them down and minimize their effectiveness. Few things excite me more than helping these charities to be freed up to do what they do best.

My personal passion is to facilitate the advancement of churches and charities so they can move from where they are to where they want to be. My hope is that in reading this book you will have a better idea as to the right questions to be asking, which in turn increases the likelihood of arriving at the right answers. This will free you to serve with greater effectiveness and efficiency so that what you do will make a difference.

?

Question #1

How Does a Charity Start?

Reasons Why a Charity is Founded

"Mommy, Daddy... can we get a puppy? I promise I'll feed it and take it for walks and play with it."

Ah, but experienced pet-owning parents know better. The novelty quickly gives way to being a nuisance. A man's best friend is replaced by "best friends forever" and good intentions are derailed by addictive video games. The child was told about the importance of making sure that the dog comes from a qualified kennel, has its shots, wears its license, is fed and watered regularly and taken for the mandatory walks and runs. But there is a significant gap between getting the information and fulfilling the obligations that are required of a responsible dog owner. Then of course there are the invitations to Grandma's house, where their beloved pet's name doesn't show up on the invitation. Who looks after the dog now? And what about those trips to the vet? Somehow the generous health benefit program provided by Dad or Mom's employer doesn't include Fido.

CHARITIES REQUIRE ONGOING CARE AND ATTENTION

Charities are not entirely unlike owning a dog. There are some stark similarities between the breeding, birth and ongoing health of the family dog and looking after a registered Charity. It is more than just a quick trip to the local breeder of charities and picking out the Charity you want. It involves the development of purposes for the Charity that must be deemed acceptable to the Charities Directorate—the government department that oversees charities. Then, there are the accompanying bylaws that spell out, in agonizing detail, every conceivable contingency and how it is to be handled. How long must an Annual General Meeting (AGM) go on without a quorum, where must an AGM be held, how much notice must be given to the Members and what happens if they aren't given proper notice? These are details that make lawyers drool with excitement while the rest of us drool while we sleep.

Throughout the book I will only be talking about registered charities, which are those that are officially registered with the government and authorized to issue tax-deductible receipts for donations received. Later on we will look at the implications of registering a Charity.

There is nothing to stop an individual or group from starting up a Charity that will dispense used clothing or operate a pre-school out of their home or their local community club without registering as a Charity. The only reason a Charity is registered is for the financial benefit gained by providing tax-deductible receipts to its donors.

WHOSE IDEA WAS THIS?

You may be currently involved with a Charity and wondering how it got started and how it got to where it is today. We are going to look at the two main reasons for starting a Charity. There will be iterations of these two reasons, but without getting too close to the brink of over-simplification, let me reduce the motivations down to two.

Charities are typically launched either by a group or an entrepreneur. For example, the drive to launch an inner-city mission, para-church organization or a church begins when an interested group gels around

> The only reason a Charity is registered is for the financial benefit gained by providing tax-deductible receipts to its donors.

an idea or a forward-thinking, ambitious individual sees that something needs to be done. How a Charity evolves is often reflective of whether its genesis was the idea of a group or just one ambitious individual.

THE GROUP APPROACH

The *Group Approach* to beginning a Charity can involve a small group of people who come together because they have a common interest in seeing a social or spiritual need met. Here is one possible scenario.

It's kind of like, "Where does love begin?"

A small group of long-time friends are sitting around having coffee one evening. In the course of conversation, they talk about the real need for a soup kitchen in an area of their city that is without such a resource. What starts out as a casual conversation imperceptibly becomes a dream. The dream begins to morph into a vision—a picture of what could happen. It's like friends who meet for coffee with no thoughts of marriage, but whose relationship at some point crosses the indiscernible line of "Why would I marry this person?" to "Why would I not?" For a Charity, a similar dividing line can be crossed from "How could we create such a place?" to "Why couldn't we create such a place?"

> Charities are typically launched either by a group or an entrepreneur.

Eventually the vision begins to take on some clarity. At that point, someone around the table realizes this could be too huge an undertaking for their liking. That *someone* looks at their watch, turns to their spouse and says, "I think it's time to go; I have a big day ahead of me." That *someone* has begun to look at the logistics and realizes it's not feasible or practical and is terrified that others in the group are less insightful and… well… simply naïve. The rest hang around until the evening concludes with an agreement to meet again and talk about the idea.

The Caring Kitchen is Conceived

At subsequent meetings, the group realizes the project will be hard work and fraught with obstacles, but everyone agrees to start small. One of the members of the group has a friend who owns some rundown retail space. They agree to talk to their friend about letting the group use the space every Friday and Saturday evening from six to eight o'clock for the purpose of inviting indigent and homeless people to drop in for sandwiches, donuts and coffee. After some phone calls and more than a few twists and bends along the way, a suitable space is acquired. Another member of the group offers to pick up a large coffee urn, while someone else agrees to pick up coffee, milk and sugar. Someone else has connections to a local bakery that will provide day-old donuts for free. Another person uses their business photocopier to run off some flyers and posters. A launch date is set and *The Caring Kitchen* is opened.

Their anxious curiosity quickly changes to panic. The initiative is so well received that on the very first night, within forty minutes of opening, they have completely run out of donuts. Making sure this does not happen on Saturday night, they double the order. Already the news has spread in the streets that there is a place where the hungry and homeless can eat. The result is double the patrons such that in less than an hour all the food is gone again. The latecomers settle for the results of an emergency run to the nearest donut shop and wait while more fresh coffee is made.

"Now what do we do?" the team asks. It is obvious they have touched on a huge need that requires a greater resource of money and time than they had originally anticipated. Keep in mind that our caring friends still have a life. They have jobs, homes and families and other ongoing commitments that do not allow them to pursue the idea of a seven-days-a-week soup kitchen, even though their hearts have been touched by the need. And then there is the pragmatic challenge relating to the cost of a facility and the food.

But they are not ready to bail on their dream, so they push forward with limited resources while they talk together about alternatives. If this need is to come anywhere close to being met, they will need a larger building and volunteers with the time and talents to operate such a facility. This will require far more money than all their disposable funds put together.

As the initiative haltingly moves forward, the original group begins to drift in opposite directions. Some of the original launch team start to lose their passion while others become more committed. Their friends hear about it and agree they would be willing to periodically volunteer.

Over time, there are individuals in the group who take on more of a leadership role. Those individuals make most of the decisions and fill in the vacant slots on the volunteer schedule. No one is formally "in" or "out" but the members of the group can be identified with a fair degree of certainty. This informal membership of fifteen individuals agrees to meet and talk about how they will move forward more formally. The outcome of the meeting sees four people volunteering to do some legwork about formalizing *The Caring Kitchen*. This also means that the remaining eleven people just got their life back. *The Four* connect at the end of the meeting to schedule their own meeting to discuss how to move forward. The four noble volunteers identify themselves as a committee, but because we know a little about charities we can already see them as the preliminary Board of Directors.

The purpose of *The Four* is to translate the wishes of the rest of the group into actions. They begin carving up the immediate tasks. Along with the ongoing responsibilities of maintaining the soup kitchen, they see the need to acquire a more permanent location at a highly discounted rate, along with getting the local food handling licenses required by the city. There is one other major responsibility—that of raising funds for the ever-expanding venture. It is the upbeat optimist of *The Four* who agrees to take on this challenge, because they know many well-heeled people who can be called on to share their wealth with the needy.

The Caring Kitchen has become a bona fide unregistered Charity. I will describe this venture using governance terms such as "Members" and "Directors," while our philanthropic friends still refer to themselves individually as volunteers and holistically as a committee.

A week after their initial meeting, they meet to bring each other up to date on their progress. One of the Directors has a formal lease in hand while a second Director knows the process for acquiring a Food Handlers License. However, the balloon of optimism is punctured by the fundraiser who tells the rest of the group about the first meeting with a prospective donor. It was an easy sell for the first ten minutes of the conversation, until the inevitable question was asked: "Will my donation be tax-deductible?"

Their passionate energy is quickly redirected toward the task of establishing a registered Charity. With thousands of charities out there, starting one up can't be all that difficult. The online application forms are downloaded and submitted and rejected, resubmitted and rejected again. By this time,

The Four recognize the need to engage some professional help to submit their application.

Eventually the original group is identified as the founding Members of the Charity. The membership is quick to rubberstamp the very first Board of Directors to oversee the operations of *The Caring Kitchen*. In time, the purposes and the bylaws of the Charity are accepted, the charitable donation number is received and donations are receipted.

> A growing Charity will eventually outstrip the capacities of a volunteer Board to manage the day-to-day activities of the Charity.

The Caring Kitchen continues to move along. Members and Directors alike agree that while they knew there was a need out there for the service they are providing, they never anticipated the magnitude of the need. The entire enterprise has been encouraging both in terms of the need it is meeting and the individuals and businesses who contribute generously due in part to the tax-deductible receipt.

It is not long before a new challenge arises. The four Directors who make up the Board are now run off their feet. Yard work at home is ignored, they show up late to their children's activities and a day off is never a day off. On top of that, each one has a career and none of those careers includes expertise in running a soup kitchen. One is an electrical engineer, another is a courier driver, while one works from home and the other is a schoolteacher. With no experience in the culinary business, it is time to hire someone to run *The Caring Kitchen*.

A growing Charity will eventually outstrip the capacities of a volunteer Board to manage the day-to-day activities of the Charity.

In the interests of the brevity and clarity of our story, let's fast track the process of hiring a Leader. There is risk in making the quantum leap from a volunteer-based Charity to one that is employing someone full-time. The work involves more than just buying donuts and coffee and managing a rent-free facility. It has moved to identifying and hiring the right person who is both qualified and available. *Available* may mean someone who is willing to start by working part-time. In addition to identifying the right individual, the volunteer Board is responsible for ensuring funds are raised to pay the new employee and handing off the responsibility of leadership of a Charity that was the brainchild of a broader group.

This hypothetical, albeit realistic, example should answer the question "How did we get here?" as it relates to a Charity that starts with the *Group Approach*.

THE ENTREPRENEURIAL APPROACH

The second way a Charity can be launched is through an *Entrepreneurial Approach*. In some respects, seeing a Charity started this way is opposite to the *Group Approach*. Keep in mind, these are two of the ways in which a Charity evolves. It does not begin with a group or individual deciding on one approach or the other; nor is one approach better than the other. The Entrepreneurial Approach is less cumbersome because many of the decisions are made unilaterally. The challenge for the entrepreneurial Leader lies in understanding that the Charity is not owned by one person and that the role of the Board is to provide overall direction.

Rather than starting out as a group idea, the Charity is the dream of a visionary—someone who has the capacity to envision what a ministry could look like down the road. Not only is this person a visionary but they may also have an entrepreneurial bent. An entrepreneur is someone who likes to take on a challenge and is willing to assume the risk to see an enterprise move forward. Keep in mind that while the new Charity starts out as a dream, it will require huge doses of initiative and fortitude to overcome inertia and enough leadership charisma for the Leader to pass along the vision so that others will become involved.

Eric has spent his entire life in the restaurant business. He began as a bus boy and a server, eventually became a chef and now manages and owns various restaurants. Having done very well for himself, he realizes that over half his working life is behind him and he would like to become involved in making a difference in the lives of needy people. Currently he and his business partner Rick own a large, upscale restaurant. Eric has a meeting with Rick to tell him about an idea to open up a soup kitchen for the disadvantaged in the community. Rick has always known about Eric's soft spot for philanthropy, so while it should not have come as a complete surprise, Rick confesses that he is shocked. However, being creative business men, they come up with a plan to have Eric remain as a partner but not be involved in the day-to-day operation of the restaurant. The restaurant business has not made him independently wealthy, but he can survive on his share of the profits from the partnership.

With that in place, Eric launches a small storefront soup kitchen which he has creatively named *The Caring Kitchen*.

Like everything else he has done in life, Eric launches into this venture with unbridled enthusiasm. As he gets closer to those who are in need of a good sandwich and a hot cup of coffee, his passion only becomes deeper.

As he moves forward, Eric's passion is moderated by the pragmatics of making the venture viable. Realizing that he will not be charging for meals anymore and without a sufficient financial base to cover all the expenses himself, he knows he will need people to buy into his vision. As he approaches his current contacts, former suppliers and philanthropically minded friends, he encounters the same common question: "Is my donation tax-deductible?"

Eric understands that if he forms a charitable organization it will require a Board. He now faces the challenge that comes with including others in a Charity. Eric's experience in the business world has been marked by quick decisions made in consultation with his partner. Now he is discovering the need to include others whom Eric quietly describes as people who have "no skin in the game." However, being influential, outgoing and well connected, Eric pulls together a group of his buddies and asks if they would be willing to sit on the Board of *The Caring Kitchen*. He promises them it will only require some signatures and a couple of meetings a year, as he will be running the soup kitchen. He finds six of his friends, one of whom is his wife, to sit on the Board. When it comes to the particulars of establishing the Charity as a legal entity, Eric is willing to take care of all those details—after all, he knows a number of lawyers from his restaurant days and he will call on one of them. Working with a Board is more unwieldy than making the business deals with which he has become accustomed. It is a challenge to get everyone at the lawyer's office at the same time to sign the documents. While the process ends up taking far more time than Eric had originally anticipated, eventually *The Caring Kitchen* becomes a registered Charity.

SUMMARY

We have here two charities founded to do precisely the same work, but launched in virtually opposite ways. One started with a group of people and worked its way down to a Leader, while the second Charity started with the Leader and expanded to include a Board. In both cases the motivation to obtain charitable status is fuelled by the need to provide donors with tax-deductible receipts.

As I mentioned at the start, these two scenarios are a simple sketch of two ways a Charity can be launched. I am not suggesting that these are the only two ways or that one is better than the other—these are just two ways a Charity can be founded.

Later on we are going to pick up on these stories and look at the inherent challenges of each approach. In the next chapter I will lay out some of the pieces that make up a Charity and try to fit them together.

?

Question #2

What Are the Pieces to the Governance Puzzle?

Identifying the Roles and Fitting Them Together

IT IS THIS PART OF UNDERSTANDING THE Charity process that can be puzzling, so let me carefully lay out the pieces of the puzzle and try to put them together in a way that results in a clear picture. Remember, I am trying to use consistent vocabulary so now is the time to put a name to each piece and then put the pieces together.

MEMBERS

Remember the group that came together with an idea to start a soup kitchen which later evolved into *The Caring Kitchen*? It was their dream to see that indigent citizens of their community had a place to have something to eat and drink. It was the final version of this group which eventually became

> The Members as owners of the Charity want to ensure that the Charity maintains the focus and intention for which it was created.

the Members of the registered Charity. It was their idea, their concern, their vision and their passion that launched the Charity. It is now their Charity and they are the legal owners. In a subsequent chapter I will look at the question of *ownership* as it relates to a Charity, but for now just keep in mind the idea that it is owned by the Members. They want to make sure the soup kitchen for needy people does not evolve into business networking on Friday evenings or a video arcade for the local youth. The Members as owners of the Charity want to ensure that the Charity maintains the focus and intention for which it was created. At the same time, they do not want to become involved or even concerned about the day-to-day operation of *The Caring Kitchen*. The Members are concerned that the Charity accomplishes what it is designed to accomplish without engaging in practices that are imprudent, unethical or illegal.

You may be more familiar with the idea of membership as it relates to Members of a cooperative, a church or a labour union. People (usually very few) come together to vote

> The role of the membership is very important to seeing that the Charity stays on track.

on a variety of routine issues such as the appointment of Directors, amendments to bylaws or the acceptance of financial statements. Membership is all that and more. Hopefully you can see from the membership of *The Caring Kitchen* that the role of the membership is very important to seeing that the

Charity stays on track. Identifying Directors, authorizing changes to the bylaws and appointing an auditor are not the only responsibilities of the Members. Membership decisions are those made at the highest and broadest level of a Charity.

I can understand if this piece of the puzzle still looks confusing. We still haven't joined it to anything to see how it fits as a part of the overall picture. But before we pick up the next piece and put the Member and Director pieces together, let's take a short side trip.

THE PURPOSE OF GOVERNANCE

The word *governance* comes from the Latin word *gubernare,* which means "to guide or direct." *Gubernare* would be used specifically in the context of guiding a ship or providing dir-

> A governing body does not exist to do what it wants, but rather it always governs, guides and directs on behalf of others.

ection for the captain. This word has evolved into what we understand today as *governance.* A governing body does not exist to do what it wants, but rather it always governs, guides and directs on behalf of others.

DIRECTORS, BOARD AND BOARD OF DIRECTORS

In this section it is particularly important to use vocabulary carefully. A common term used to describe Directors is *board members.* There is nothing wrong with that term, but to minimize the confusion between *board members* and the *Members* of the Charity, when I use the term *Board,* I am referring to the group of Directors, more commonly referred to as the *Board of*

Directors. It is the *individual* Directors that make up the Board of Directors or what I will refer to as the *Board*.

The Members of the Charity are individuals who have an overall desire to see a benefit achieved for an identifiable group of people, but realize they cannot do it all themselves. As such, Members will select from among themselves Directors who will ensure that the wishes of the Members are carried out.

> The role of the Board is to govern the Charity on behalf of the Members who are the owners, to ensure that the Charity's objectives, as established by the founders and supported by the Members, are carried out.

The role of the Board is to govern the Charity on behalf of the Members who are the owners, to ensure that the Charity's objectives, as established by the founders and supported by the Members, are carried out. The Board is not the "boss" of the Charity. Its purpose is to serve the Members by understanding the ongoing interests and concerns of the Members and ensure those interests and concerns take place at an operational level. The interest of the Members may want to see that homeless people are cared for with dignity and respect. Operational details could include how to address intoxicated individuals who want to have a bed for the night or how often mattresses are replaced.

What the Board is Not

The position of the Board is not a power position, having the authority to move the Charity in whatever direction it wishes.

The Board needs to constantly check with the Members to ensure the ship is going in the right direction.

It is not the job of the Board or of any single Director to support and assist the Leader. The role of the Board has nothing to do with supporting the Leader. To be clear: the Board *ought* to support the Leader, but that is not its role.

If I ask you how you see your role if you are a parent, you will likely respond by saying it is one of guiding and directing your children in a healthy and positive direction. You would also agree that your primary role is not to keep your children happy, try as they might to persuade you otherwise. If it was, their happiness would override your commitment to guide and discipline them. Are you concerned that your children are happy? Of course you are. Should you be disturbed if they are not happy? Yes. However, ensuring their happiness is not your primary role. In the same way a Board will want to be supportive of its Leader, it must not do so at the expense of its primary role which is to ensure the Charity moves in the desired direction of the Members.

> The role of the Board has nothing to do with supporting the Leader.

It is not the task of the Board to manage the Leader or see itself as part of the management team. The Board must be closely linked to the Members to understand the intentions of the Members and then report to the Members that those intentions are being realized. Using our analogy of the puzzle, the Director piece needs to interlock with the Member piece.

Members and Directors Have Very Distinct Roles

You might be wondering if the Charity with which you are associated has Members. In Canada all charities have Members. In many cases the Members and the Directors are the same individuals. It is important for individuals who are filling both roles to make sure they are wearing the right uniform for the right job.

Reference is sometimes made to a self-perpetuating Board. Technically speaking there is no such thing as a self-perpetuating Board. What you *can* have is a Charity with a set number of Members who appoint themselves as the Directors. For example the original group that launched *The Caring Kitchen* could just as easily have been a group of six people who became the founding Members and appointed themselves to the Board of Directors.

The advantage of having a membership of forty or fifty people allows for a broader ownership of the Charity. There are potentially more people who can be drawn on to raise support, provide donations, volunteer and have as potential Directors.

The advantage of having a fixed number of Members all serving as Directors is the increased likelihood of having long-term passionate Directors, which provides Board stability. There is no need to educate and contextualize new Directors to the workings of the Board or bring them up to speed.

So what is to prevent Directors from becoming set in their ways and unwilling to give up their position on the Board? One solution is to have the Members appoint Directors every year or to establish term limitations. That way when a Director becomes more of a liability than an asset, that Director can be replaced. Of course, it is easier said than done when the same Directors have been together for a long time. Thus you can see the advantage to having a larger membership that serves as a pool from which to draw new Directors when either the term or capabilities of current Directors has expired.

THE ANNUAL GENERAL MEETING

At the Annual General Meeting (AGM), Members have the opportunity to speak as a group. They can elect Directors as well as provide input into other decisions, ensuring the objectives of the Charity are maintained.

As mentioned earlier, AGMs are traditionally not well attended. One reason is that Members do not believe their input is considered, never mind valued. One of the ways to change the function of an AGM is to move away from an agenda-driven meeting to one in which the primary purpose is to get feedback from the Members. Of course, certain functions must take place such as the appointment of Directors. Nonetheless, when the primary focus of the AGM is to hear from Members, the potential of increased attendance, and therefore increased involvement, is heightened.

THE LEADER

While a Charity must have Members and Directors, it is not required to have a Leader. Remember that I am using the term "Leader" synonymously with "Executive Director" or "CEO." In some cases the Leader may be one of the Directors;

however, as we continue to identify the pieces, I will assume
the Leader to be someone employed full-time by the Board.

> The term *Leader* is used
> to describe the one
> person hired by the
> Board to whom the
> Board has delegated
> the responsibility to
> ensure that what should
> happen, happens, and
> what should not happen
> does not happen.

The term *Leader* is used to
describe the one person hired
by the Board to whom the Board
has delegated the responsibility
to ensure that what should happen, happens, and what should
not happen does not happen.
The Leader executes the plan—
hence the commonly used
title *"executive* Director." This
should not be confused with Directors who sit on the Board.
Executive Director refers to the person who executes the delegated authority of the Board. Later on we will flesh out the
details as to how this is done, but for now it is important to
remember that the Leader is the only employee who reports
directly to the Board.

EMPLOYEES

Employees are hired by the Leader to carry out the day-to-
day operations of the Charity. Employees report directly or
indirectly to the Leader, but should never be required to report to the Board. Later I will talk about why it is important
that a Director does not make an end run on the Leader by
giving advice or eliciting information from an employee. The
only employee with whom the Board formally interacts is the
Leader. This should not be taken to mean that a Director cannot talk with an employee, go for coffee with them or show

a personal interest in their life. In the event a connection of that type is made, it is vital that both the Director and the employee are aware of the nature of the interaction. It would be helpful as well for the Leader to be aware of such a connection so there is no perception that the interaction crosses any lines of authority.

VOLUNTEERS

Very few charities can function without volunteers. In fact, volunteers are just assumed. In 2006, the Canadian Volunteerism Institute developed an audit tool called *The Canadian Code for Volunteer Involvement*[x], pointing to the development

> Employees report directly or indirectly to the Leader, but should never be required to report to the Board.

of more and more resources to assist charities in relating to volunteers, valuing both their contribution in terms of the work they do as well as the wisdom and perspective they bring.

When a Member or Director volunteers to do work other than in their role as a Member or Director, they do so only as volunteers and as such should never use or confuse their role as a Member or a Director to exercise influence over the Leader.

MORAL OWNERS

Earlier we talked about the Members being the legal owners of the Charity. A Charity also has *Moral Owners* who have an interest in the success and impact of the Charity. One example

When a Member or Director volunteers to do work other than in their role as a Member or Director, they do so only as volunteers and as such should never use or confuse their role as a Member or a Director to exercise influence over the Leader.

of a Moral Owner is someone who donates to a Charity. A donation of $20 does not entitle them to a vote at an AGM nor does a donation of $20,000 suggest they should be given consideration as a Director. Nevertheless, their money has been given to advance the purposes of the Charity and to that extent they have moral ownership. An example of a Moral Owner who has become more prevalent is that of a church adherent who is not a Member of the church. They will describe the church as "their church," may donate regularly and volunteer significantly, but not be a Member given the working definition I have provided thus far. These people are Moral Owners and as such, their input needs to be sought out and given consideration by the Directors. Do not confuse this with non-members being allowed to incessantly complain.

STAKEHOLDERS

This is a term that has recently come into greater use. A Stakeholder is simply someone who has a stake in the Charity. Let me differentiate between Stakeholders and Moral Owners. Moral Owners have a direct interest regarding the impact that the Charity has on those who benefit from it. Someone can be a Stakeholder without being a Member or a Moral Owner. Going back to *The Caring Kitchen*, one of the significant Stakeholders would be the landlord. The landlord cares whether donations come in or if the Charity continues to exist. The success or existence of the Charity has a direct impact on the landlord. Beyond that, the landlord may not have any personal concern regarding the impact the Charity has on its beneficiaries. The same is true as it relates to the wholesaler from whom the Charity purchases its cups and napkins or the bakery that supplies the buns and donuts.

Every Moral Owner is a Stakeholder, but not every Stakeholder is a Moral Owner.

PUTTING THE PIECES TOGETHER

As it relates to governance, the three key pieces are the Members, the Board and the Leader. Let's take these three pieces and see how they fit together.

Suppose you and your spouse are in your late forties and have never been on a winter vacation. Now that you have a little more disposable income you decide you want to go somewhere warm for a week. You begin by calling a travel agent, saying that you want to go somewhere that is warm and has a nice sandy beach. You want to go for one week and want your trip to be an all-inclusive plan such that your travel, accommodations and meals are included in the trip. Oh, and you don't want to pay more than $4,000. You have just described a preferred destination within the parameters of specific criteria. You don't care which all-inclusive beach resort you go to as long as the criteria are met. That is essentially the role of the Members: they describe the destination.

The travel agent then takes your wishes (aka criteria) and

gives overall direction to those wishes. The agent has no right to redefine the destination by booking a four-day trip to Las Vegas. They are only allowed to interpret your wishes and ensure those wishes are realized. In the same way a travel agent gives overall direction so the desired destination can be reached, a Board needs to understand the desires of the Members and make the arrangements so that the desires of the Members are met.

The travel agent does not take care of every detail. They do not hire maids to clean your room or servers to bring your dinner or pilots to fly the plane.

> The Members define the destination, the Board provides the direction and the Leader executes the details.

They are more likely to engage the services of a tour company who looks after all those details. The tour company serves a similar role to the Leader.

The Members define the destination, the Board provides the direction and the Leader executes the details.

Each piece of a puzzle is different and each piece is important. If one puzzle piece is forced into a space where it doesn't belong there will be two problems. First the picture will be muddled and second there will be a piece that doesn't fit anywhere else.

The same is true with the governance of a Charity. Members, Directors and the Leader need to understand the purpose and importance of their roles and fill those roles well so the Charity can perform the function for which it was created.

Summary

In this chapter we have given a name to each piece, laid out those pieces and seen how the pieces fit together to complete the governance puzzle; but we have left out one important detail. Each registered Charity has a partner it needs to constantly consider and to whom it is accountable. In our next chapter we will find out who that is and why charities need this partner.

?

Question #3

Why is There So Much Government Involvement?

The Government as a Partner

IF YOU HAVE HAD EXPERIENCE WITH A Canada Revenue Agency (CRA) audit of a Charity, you may want to replace the word *involvement* with *interference*.

On the other hand, if you've not had any experience with the government and its relationship to a Charity, you may be wondering why anyone would take the government in as a partner. But in fact, there are some good reasons.

The government recognizes the importance of charities, and that is good news! A registered Charity is a structure that is set up because the government realizes it cannot do everything for everybody. Society has gaps both nationally and internationally that the government recognizes need to be filled. In light of this need, CRA grants qualified organizations a charitable tax status under the terms of the Income Tax Act (ITA). This allows a Charity to issue donation receipts to those who donate to that Charity. In this case *The Caring Kitchen* used the expertise of its lawyer to obtain registered Charity status. Note that an organization is created first, and only then can it apply for charitable status. It is a two-step process.

While some might suggest that true Charity doesn't care whether it's tax deductible or not, in Canada the savings are quite significant.

Let's have a very basic look at this from a high level. When someone makes a donation to a registered Charity, that Charity can issue a receipt to the donor, which can be used to reduce the amount of income tax the donor is required to pay. The tax credit varies somewhat from province to province, but regardless, the savings are significant. These considerations are subject to change with any federal government budget, but the numbers have been fairly consistent over the past number of years. Keep in mind: this book is not designed to interpret the ITA, replace or imitate the *Charities Handbook* published by the Canadian Council of Christian Charities, or take the place of professional advice from an accountant.

> While some might suggest that true Charity doesn't care whether it's tax deductible or not, in Canada the savings are quite significant.

Donations to registered charities result in a tax credit, which means the donor receives a direct credit against their tax payable. It is not based on their tax bracket or marginal tax rate. When the federal and provincial taxes are combined, the average taxpayer can reduce their taxes by about 25% on the first $200 donated and the savings are about 45% on the remaining amount contributed.

The benefits of charitable status and charitable giving can be easily noted in this interesting exercise.

Find an online tax program.

> When the federal and provincial taxes are combined, the average taxpayer can reduce their taxes by about 25% on the first $200 donated and the savings are about 45% on the remaining amount contributed.

- Enter an annual gross income of $1 million
  - Note the tax payable without a donation
  - Enter a $100,000 donation (10% of the gross income)
  - Find out what the tax savings are
- Enter an annual gross income of $50,000
  - Note the tax payable without a donation
  - Enter a $5,000 donation (10% of the gross income)
  - Find out what the tax savings are
- Enter an annual gross income of $20,000
  - Note the tax payable without a donation
  - Enter a $2,000 donation (10% of the gross income)
  - Find out what the tax savings are

The tax credit on donations at each level will be close to 45%.

While a registered Charity does not benefit directly from this provision, it is clear that the willingness of people to contribute can be significantly influenced by knowing they will receive close to 45 cents back on every dollar they donate over $200. Registered charities are correct in believing they will receive more donations at higher amounts if they are a registered Charity that can issue receipts to its donors.

Why is the Government is a Partner?

The Charity has essentially invited the government to be a partner in their Charity by the 45% savings to the donor.

> The Charity has essentially invited the government to be a partner in their Charity by the 45% savings to the donor.

Consider that the government gives 45 cents back to the donor for every dollar that is contributed; therefore the government has 45 cents less in its coffers. (Of course, we know that the government does not have any money other than what it receives in countless ways from its citizens.) The government must then consider how it is going to raise the 45 cents it refunded to the donor. It will do that by receiving money from taxpayers through other means. A donor to *The Caring Kitchen* has affected non-donating taxpayers because the government is providing tax considerations to those who donate to *The Caring Kitchen*. Rightly so, the government wants to be confident that *The Caring Kitchen* is using donor dollars wisely by accomplishing its declared mission of seeing that hungry people are fed. In this way the government is not only a partner, it is a regulator. *The*

Caring Kitchen cannot provide charitable services that do not align with its purposes. For example, it has declared it will provide food for people in the local area and as such is not allowed to support an aid worker in Afghanistan.

Get the Scoop on Every Registered Charity in Canada

The government acquires a lot of necessary information from its "Charity partners" through an annual return. Because taxpayers are the ones affected by the tax savings provided by the government, that information is readily available. The summary of a Charity's return is accessible online at www. cra-arc.gc.ca/chrts-gvng/lstngs/menu-eng.html. There you can find information about your favourite (or not so favourite!) Charity, such as who sits on the Board, how much money it received, how much was spent on fundraising—all the way down to how much was spent on bank charges and interest.

Summary

In the previous chapter I laid out most of the pieces: seeing how Members, the Board and the Leader fit together. In this chapter I described the benefits for registering a Charity and the challenges that come with those benefits. We can conclude that the CRA is not just a silent partner standing on the sidelines, but a partner involved in the details of all registered charities.

Question #4

Who Owns a Charity?

A Unique Concept of Ownership

"IT'S MINE!"

It didn't take any of us long to learn that phrase. The only difference between a two-year-old and a forty-two-year-old is the price of the toy.

Ownership is a well-understood western concept. Because I have legal ownership of something, I am entitled to pretty much treat it the way I want. I can paint the rooms in my house black or use a broom to paint my car purple. I can sell what I own for whatever price the purchaser is willing to pay. In the case of my house with the black rooms and my poorly painted purple car, the market may be limited, but there will always be a buyer at the right price. In the business world there are publicly traded companies. Millions of shares in publicly traded companies are bought and sold every day at a mutually agreed upon price by the buyer and the seller. In a similar way, my house, my car, my business and the shares I own in other businesses are assets. My assets can be sold for cash, which I can then take and convert into another asset.

Legal ownership of a Charity is somewhat different. First of all, a Charity does not have shares that can be bought and sold.

> A Charity does not have shares that can be bought and sold.

Suppose the government was to set up a program whereby it would provide a free Rototiller to any homeowner who was willing to plough up their backyard and plant vegetables. The produce would then be given to a government-registered food bank. It clearly makes more sense to use one's backyard for something valuable like providing food for the poor rather than have it sown to grass that has no nutritional benefit. However, there might be some conditions to this government offer.

First: the Rototiller could only be used to plough up an area which would be used for vegetables which in turn would be given to a food bank approved by the government. It could not be used to plough my own vegetable garden or my flower garden at the end of the season.

Second: the Rototiller could not be used to generate income by ploughing up the neighbour's garden, unless they were also going to give all the vegetables to the government food bank.

To be absolutely clear on this: the government would give me a Rototiller free of charge provided I used it only for the purpose for which it was intended. I would not benefit from the Rototiller nor could I sell it to anyone else.

Would I own the Rototiller? Yes, because my name would be on the bill of sale. It would be my responsibility to keep it in good repair, buy gas to keep it running and store it. Furthermore, if a child came along, grabbed the hot muffler and burned their hand (perish the thought), I am the one who would be sued.

Next question: In this scenario, is this Rototiller my own asset? No, it is not. An asset is something of economic value that I own and can be converted to cash. I own the Rototiller that is taking up space in my garage and can only be used for a charitable purpose. But it is not an asset. It has no value other than being used for the purposes for which it was intended, which is to provide vegetables for the less fortunate. If I decided I wanted to convert the vegetable garden back to a lawn, plant flowers, use it to grow vegetables for myself or use it for a dog run, I would be free to do that. I could return the Rototiller to the *Department of Rototillers* (I hope no creative politician is reading this!) or fill out some forms and give the Rototiller to a neighbour who agreed to use it subject to the same government conditions. But *my* Rototiller would not be an asset.

There is no condition on what kind of vegetables need to be grown or if I have to grow anything at all. Of course, there is no use having a Rototiller that will just take up space in my garage if it is not going to be used for its intended purpose. But there is nothing to prevent me from having a Rototiller purchased by the government.

Like any analogy, this one will have its flaws, but hopefully it serves to distinguish between the ideas of *ownership* and *assets*.

A Charity can *have* assets but the Charity itself *is not* an asset. It can own buildings, furnishings, equipment and vehicles; however, none of those assets can be sold with the proceeds accruing to the Members. Unlike a house or a car which belongs to its owner, assets of a Charity do not belong to its Members.

> A Charity can *have* assets but the Charity itself *is not* an asset.

We keep coming back to the idea that a Charity has a clearly stated purpose. People who serve on a Board often have a business or entrepreneurial background and as such have a challenge getting hold of the idea that a Charity is different than a for-profit business. They are often not used to dealing with shareholders, which are the equivalent of Members of a Charity. They may not be used to the amount of government regulation. Directors are only trustees of the Charity, with a responsibility to the Members. The Members in one respect are owners, but they do not have the same rights that we would traditionally consider the rights of an owner. A Charity does not exist for the benefit of its Members.

> A Charity does not exist for the benefit of its Members. It can only be used for the purpose for which it was originally designated.

It can only be used for the purpose for which it was originally designated. The purpose or purposes are those that were stated in the letters patent at the time the Charity was registered.

Unlike a business, a Charity cannot be bought, sold or
arbitrarily taken over. There are
conditions under which a Char-

> A Charity always exists
> for the benefit of others.

ity can merge with an existing Charity if the two charities
have identical objectives. I won't go into any further detail
here as that topic is outside the scope of this book.

We talked about the concept of Moral Ownership in the
previous chapter. However, I cannot overstate the importance of understanding that a Charity always exists for the
benefit of others.

You can see the importance of balancing the concept of
ownership. On one hand the Members are the owners of the
Charity in somewhat the same way as a homeowner can own
a Rototiller which can only be used for charitable purposes.
On the other hand, ownership of a Charity cannot be confused with the notion that ownership constitutes an asset.

SUMMARY

We have looked at the idea of ownership as it relates to a
Charity. We have seen that it is different from the typical way
in which we view ownership. It can take some time and reflection for this concept to take hold.

Early on in the book, we saw two different ways that *The
Caring Kitchen* could have been launched. While it was getting established, we took some time off to get an understanding of how all the pieces of a Charity fit together. We discov-
ered that the Members own the Charity—sort of. We found
out that the assets of *The Caring Kitchen* can't be sold and the

proceeds divided among the Members. We have seen that the Members appointed a Board of Directors that is charged with ensuring *The Caring Kitchen* continues on the course desired by the Members. We are grateful for all those who put so much work into this charitable venture as it has continued to grow and have a significant impact on the poor and homeless—so much so that a Leader has been hired.

In our next chapter we are going to visit *The Caring Kitchen* to see how they are doing under the *Group Approach* and the *Entrepreneurial Approach*. I am guessing that within both scenarios everyone has encountered some choppy waters.

?

Question #5

Who's In Charge of a Charity?

Understanding the Role of the Board and the Leader

WHILE YOU AND I HAVE HAD OUR FEET UP reading this book, our friends at *The Caring Kitchen* have had their sleeves rolled up running the soup kitchen. Some of those sleeves have been literally rolled up by volunteers in the kitchen, while the sleeves of the Board and the Leader have been figuratively rolled up as they each work through their role in the Charity.

In chapter one we saw that under both the Group Approach and the Entrepreneurial Approach, *The Caring Kitchen* was registered as a Charity to enable it to issue tax receipts. As we know, these receipts allow for a significant financial benefit. Many people have donated funds to this venture that they otherwise may have donated elsewhere had the tax benefit not been available.

Like our family dog in chapter one, the Charity needs to be taken care of. It cannot be conceived, birthed and then left in a corporate kennel, never to be cared for again. Charities need to be well-governed, well-managed and highly valued both by the Members and the Board of the Charity.

> The Charity needs to be taken care of. It cannot be conceived, birthed and then left in a corporate kennel, never to be cared for again.

As you read this book you may have a particular Charity in mind — like your current place of worship that has been in existence for a long time. In that church there may be long-term Members who have seen countless short-term pastors come and go. Or you might be overwhelmed as a Director of a small Charity that has recently registered with the government. Maybe your Charity has a Leader who seems to carry the Charity on their back by essentially doing what they want with the predictable approval of the Board.

Whatever your example or circumstance, keep it in mind as we see how a Charity can drift over time from the original intention to a current circumstance which barely resembles the original idea.

When working with charities, one of the first things I want to see is any document that pertains to how the Charity was founded as well as its current bylaws. You should not be surprised to know that many charities would be hard-pressed to find some of the founding documents. The last anyone knew, old Mr. Picadilly had them and he has been dead for years or the long-time Board Secretary has moved to the South Pacific. I like to see what the bylaws say regarding how the Charity is intended to operate and if it is operating in compliance with those bylaws. I cannot over emphasize the importance of understanding how a Charity was founded and seeing if it functions in alignment with those documents.

A problem is never a problem until it's a problem. If your house has a cracked foundation, that will not be a problem until a door jams or water begins to leak into your basement. Charities have the same challenges. Certain bylaws are ignored or the role of the Board is minimized or the responsibilities of the Leader are unclear. A Charity can drift along for a long time without those cracks becoming evident. Sadly, by the time they do become evident there is often so much damage that repairs become very painful and costly.

Many Boards have a great working relationship with their Leader. The Board understands its role and the relationship it has with its Leader. The Leader is clear regarding their function along with the responsibilities and accountability that go with that function.

Unfortunately such is not always the case. Any time there is a lack of clarity regarding the role of the Board and the role of the Leader, it is *always* the fault of the Board. We will elaborate on this in subsequent chapters.

> Any time there is a lack of clarity regarding the role of the Board and the role of the Leader, it is *always* the fault of the Board.

For now we will look at two extremes that a Board can move toward as it seeks to govern. With that in mind we will look at the two ways in which *The Caring Kitchen* began and the ways in which it can drift.

A Visit with the Group

Let's sit down with the original group who passionately launched *The Caring Kitchen.* As the founding Members, they enthusiastically tell us about their first meeting, including who all was there. One Member of the group even has the napkins on which the original plans were sketched. The four original Directors talk about the first love that everyone had to see this ministry launched. They reminisce about the times they worked until two in the morning building tables and counters, recalling the patrons who stuffed sandwiches and donuts into their well-worn parkas as they left. Ahh… the good old days. While we smile at their growing pains, we begin to understand some of their current challenges.

So how are things now?

"Things are going well… for the most part. Of course there are the usual challenges of any mission," we are told. One Director points out that hiring and keeping a good Leader is the greatest challenge because it requires the greatest amount of attention and consumes far too much of their time.

They had courted and hired a Leader. In the beginning it was wonderful, but the honeymoon was brief. Exhausted from launching this venture, the group was only too glad to offload all the responsibilities of the Charity onto the newly hired Leader. It was wonderful to have someone with lots of experience and expertise which no one on the Board possessed. Before long, the ideas the Board had put in place were described as "primitive" and set aside. The Leader explained to the Board that the only way to have an effective ministry would be to significantly ramp up the size and quality of the soup kitchen location and expand the program.

At first blush the Directors thought this sounded like a great idea, and who were they to argue? At the same time, they just didn't feel comfortable with the direction this was going—a discomfort they were unable to articulate. As the conversation continues, we discover that the difficulty is less about the Board being unable to articulate its concerns and more about it being *unwilling* to articulate them. The Board fears that if it addresses its concerns, the Leader will quit. It knows the Leader has frequent invitations to serve elsewhere with better pay and staying with *The Caring Kitchen* is a financial and professional sacrifice. As a result the Board has handled its discomfort by becoming increasingly disengaged from the Leader given the experience and expertise and the common knowledge that jumping ship was an option.

You and I have left that meeting feeling sad for the Board and somewhat annoyed with the Leader; although in fairness, the Leader was not there to provide a defence.

So we go for coffee and debrief. We begin to see the likelihood of this drifting in one of two directions.

Drifting Toward Rubberstamping

Passive indifference will be the first wind to push this ship off course. The Board has gone through the process of hiring a Leader and is not interested in facing the challenge again anytime soon. The Board as we know it will likely remain disengaged indefinitely or until a crisis develops.

The crisis could possibly arrive when the financial deficit becomes untenable.

When the Charity is finally spinning out of control, the Board will then become reactive. It may remove the Leader (assuming the ship has not already been abandoned), who is deemed to be the problem. Once the Board realizes that removing the "problem" is not a long-term solution, it may hire another Leader. There are times when a Board realizes it needs to remove a Leader and hire a different Leader. However, far too often this is done in response to a chronic problem or a crisis rather than a carefully contemplated decision.

Drifting Toward Micromanagement

The second drift off course takes the ship in the opposite direction if the Board reacts by micromanaging—all the while becoming resentful and distrustful of the Leader. Going forward, every detail will require the approval of the Board.

A Board like this can be made up of Directors who originally started the Charity or who have been on the Board for many years and as such hang on tightly to the reins of control. It sees the role of the Leader as little more than a paid assistant whose job it is to carry out the wishes of the Board. These wishes are often communicated in an ad hoc and capacious manner. The Leader is supposed to order the coffee, only to have their fingers rapped for failing to buy Fair Trade coffee, even though it is more expensive and the mandate is to keep expenses to a minimum. The Leader's failure to avoid the administrative landmines eventually leads to their dismissal unless they are smart enough to leave before that happens.

The same thing can happen in churches—particularly in smaller churches. Members of these churches typically have a high degree of ownership where their church is concerned, which in itself is not a bad thing; but watch what can happen.

The church has a man in his forties who is a long-time Member. His parents, grandparents and a variety of relatives were all Members. Some have since passed on but their influence remains. Disgruntled with the pastor and not seeing the changes he wants, this long-time Member announces, "I was here before this pastor came and I will be here long after he's gone." The pastor is fully aware that he cannot make any decisions except those he is supposed to make and he is never sure which ones those are. He was challenged to do more than he ought to be doing and reprimanded for doing what he should not be doing. He should have figured that out after all the knuckle rapping; however, an even bigger challenge is the moving target of Board and church expectations. Eventually he resigns, having failed to successfully lead even a small church and therefore with little hope of leading a significantly larger church. After four years of Bible college and some seminary training, he turns his back on the pastorate and enrols in a truck driver training school. All that is left of his ministry are exhaust fumes.

The Board that adopts the "it's my Charity" attitude will invariably keep its Leader in check until that Leader resigns. Any subsequent Leader who goes into a situation like this is either a passive administrative assistant type or an individual who does not have the skills to lead the Charity. In that case the Leader will eventually be asked to move on.

A Charity will never achieve its potential impact until it has a visionary Board that is willing to release the day-to-day operations to a competent Leader.

AN OVERDUE MEETING WITH THE ENTREPRENEUR

> A Charity will never achieve its potential impact until it has a visionary Board that is willing to release the day-to-day operations to a competent Leader.

What are the potential crosswinds for charities that are started by an entrepreneur like our friend Eric the restaurateur-turned-philanthropist? Remember, he has done all the legwork in getting the Board started by recruiting his friends. He assured them that their role would be perfunctory. They all met at the lawyer's office, signed some documents and left with Eric making an offhand comment about calling a meeting sometime in the near future. *The Caring Kitchen* is already meeting a real need in the community so there is no need for them to be involved.

Several months later…

Two of the Directors, personal friends, are having lunch together. Halfway through their pasta, one of the Directors mentions that he thinks the Board has some legal obligations as Directors of *The Caring Kitchen*. He goes on to tell the fellow Director that instead of just being requisite Directors, they are ultimately responsible for everything from ensuring the kitchen has a proper Food Handlers License to making sure the annual T3010—whatever that is—is filed with the government. While neither had given any thought to this before, since there are all kinds of charities and this can't be a big deal, they agree to mention it to Eric.

The following week they have lunch with Eric. When they float their newfound information past him, they are surprised by his pushback. Maybe this conversation is not going to be as perfunctory as they had originally thought. Eric reminds them that *The Caring Kitchen* was his idea and he had invited them to be on the Board because they were friends. Now their questions sound suspicious, unsupportive and untrusting. The more conciliatory of the two Directors tries to ratchet down the tension. "Eric, we just want to clarify the role and responsibilities we have as Directors. We value what you are doing and we want to be supportive. We just have some questions." However, Eric is not answering any of their questions in a way that would assuage their concerns. Rather he is becoming more and more defensive as they question their role as Directors of *his* ministry. Default personalities float to the surface. Both Directors quietly back away and Eric once again assumes control.

Board meetings and AGMs become annual but tedious events where forms are signed and any decisions requiring a vote of the Board are rubberstamped. The Directors with the least amount of tolerance for risk eventually resign. New Directors quickly replace their disillusioned predecessors.

A setting like this can go on for a long time, but not forever. Sooner or later, Directors who failed to do their due diligence at the outset will eventually have the governance bit firmly in their teeth. They will realize they are the governance leaders and the ultimate responsibility lies with them. The founder of the Charity, who bankrolled a large portion of the charitable venture, not to mention incalculable amounts of energy, is now being challenged and reined in by his Board. Feeling hurt, betrayed and offended he lashes out. Words like "traitor" and "backstabber" are vocabulary heard at the meetings. These situations seldom end well with neither party ever getting around to owning their contribution to the disaster.

On the part of the Board, it has been a chain jerk reaction. It is like allowing the family dog to run full tilt on its leash. Just as the dog reaches the end of its leash, the owner jerks the chain, coming just shy of breaking the dog's neck. Similarly, the Leader is the only one who does not know that they are coming very close to the end of the leash. The Board has felt powerless to control the Leader to this point and will use the chain jerk to draw them up short. The Leader has ignored or been oblivious to any of the concerns of the Board. When the end comes, the Leader will often leave devastated but without any clear awareness of their culpability in the disaster.

> The common theme in *Board versus Leader* conflict is the failure to understand the role of the Board and the role of the Leader and that failure is always a failure of the Board.

These organizational and relational disasters happen because neither the Board nor the Leader was clear regarding their role in the Charity.

We have looked at two dysfunctional Boards: one made up of Directors who viewed the Charity as "our ministry" and the Leader who will do only as told. The second is a Board in name only, passively complying with the wishes of the Leader.

We do well to ask what went wrong in each of these situations. And while each circumstance is different, there is a common theme and some common problems.

The common theme in *Board versus Leader* conflict is the failure to understand the role of the Board and the role of the Leader and that failure is always a failure of the Board.

I personally feel deep sadness when the failure of good governance distracts and potentially derails a Charity that could otherwise offer so much to so many that are so needy.

SUMMARY

Thus far we have looked closely at two Board scenarios with potentially disastrous dynamics because the role of the Board and the role of the Leader are not identified, clarified and differentiated. This happens far too often and tragically can happen more than once to the same Charity. I am confident that a disaster of this type is avoidable, but some minor tweaking of the governance process is not a solution. When a Board does what it has always done, it will eventually get what it has always gotten.

> Minor tweaking of the governance process is not a solution. When a Board does what it has always done, it will eventually get what it has always gotten.

In the next chapter we will look at an alternative to rubberstamping the Leader's decisions or micromanaging the Leader's administration.

?

Question #6

What is the Alternative to Rubberstamping or Micromanaging?

An Introduction to Policy Governance®

I RECALL ALL TOO WELL THE REGIMEN FOR writing high school exams. Classes were force-marched into the gymnasium and appropriately searched to ensure no contraband was being smuggled. We would sit stiffly at a desk while the General marched down the aisle slapping a thick document face-down on each desk. At precisely 0900 hours the inmates were allowed to turn over the classified document and commence the three-hour sentence.

I recall the envy I felt when certain students quietly got up and handed in their exam and walked out of the gymnasium—envy because the class genius had just aced another exam. Sometimes it was smug satisfaction because there was someone who knew even less than me. My objective was to see how long I could stay and how much I could write. What I responded to on the exam often had little or no correlation to the question. Some of my teachers were fans of fluff which would net me an average mark. Others were a little more— shall I say—discerning, realizing I had no clue about the question, never mind the answer.

My memory of high school exams gives me great empathy for how some Directors feel. The difference in the boardroom is this time the exams land on the desk face-up. In high school I was given the questions and expected to provide the answers. At the Board meeting the Director is given the answers and asked to provide the questions. The one common element is the amount of fluff produced by the Leader and the Board's willingness to wade through the septic field of seemingly irrelevant data. Such aimless meandering includes Directors keeping quiet when they have no understanding of the issues under discussion. The presenter of the budget will make reference to a number that is halfway down page seven on the right-hand side, which when added to the number on the left-hand side at the bottom of page three equals the number at the top of page five. Directors will nod their heads imperceptibly, each hoping they will not be singled out by a question. To be a good Director, one needs to occasionally speak up at a Board meeting by offering a passionate discourse on a subject that is near and dear to their heart, regardless of its relevance to the overall discussion. The net result of the meeting is significant time and talent wasted, minor decisions made and forty acres worth of good timber ultimately headed for the shredder.

The greatest inventions created to increase the efficiency of Board meetings have been the laptop and the smartphone. The discreet use of these inventions ensures that meetings such as the one just described are not a complete waste of time.

Recently I chatted with a friend who had been on the Board of his church for a long time. He is convinced that 90% of the decisions discussed at a Board meeting could be made just as effectively without a Board. In essence he was saying that decisions and directions were taken, irrespective of the Board's involvement. I suggested that could be good or bad depending on how he looked at it.

The role of a Board is to decide what should be done and what should not be done, and to make sure that what should be done is done and what should not be done is not done.

> The role of a Board is to decide what should be done and what should not be done, and to make sure that what should be done is done and what should not be done is not done.

Reference is sometimes made to *working* Boards—whatever that means. In small charities some of the Directors may also be involved in various volunteer activities within the Charity; but they are engaging in those activities as volunteers of the Charity and not in their role as Directors. One of the greatest challenges is to differentiate their role as a Director from their role as a volunteer.

If my friend believes that much of the work of the church could be done without the Board, I submit that he is absolutely correct and that is as it should be. If he meant that most of the day-to-day operations are done without the Board's involvement, I would again concur that such is the way it should be. However, if he understands that the Board is just there to sit back and watch the Leader, nodding in agreement or tweaking the wording of a presentation, then he would be right in saying that the Board is basically ineffective and the Directors are wasting their time.

> Sometimes we view a Board in the same way we view the appendix in our body. We aren't quite sure why it's there, but until it causes a big enough problem we leave it untouched.

Sometimes we view a Board in the same way we view the appendix in our body. We aren't quite sure why it's there, but until it causes a big enough problem we leave it untouched. Similarly, given the way many Charity Boards operate, Directors feel their input makes no difference and "surgically removing" the Board would not significantly impact the overall operation of the Charity. Because they have misunderstood their role on the Board, they will inevitably feel their input is meaningless. Boards should not be viewed as an organizational appendix that exists for its own sake. They need to understand its function and how critical it is to the life of the Charity.

One of the things I try to do when consulting with a Charity that is stuck or seems to be lost, is retrace the steps of the organization back to its beginning. In the first chapter we saw why and how *The Caring Kitchen* ended up with a Board.

In our first example—the *Group Approach—The Caring Kitchen* had a Board because it needed a smaller team to oversee the operation of the Charity. The Members originally anticipated that the Board would do a lot of the grunt work to ensure the Charity accomplished the goals of the entire membership. The point at which the Board was appointed, the Members had not anticipated the ministry growing to where it would need a hands-on Leader. In the *Entrepreneurial Approach*, the Directors originally saw themselves only as a legal requirement so their friend could launch a Charity.

Keeping in mind that the only role of the Board is to govern, we must ask the question "How does a Board govern?" One of the requirements of the Board is to connect with its Members. The Board is not an entity unto itself. It does not have the right to do what it wants or move the Charity in a direction that may not reflect the interests or the intentions of the Members. A healthy, functional Board wants to constantly keep its ear to the ground to find out what the Members want.

> The Board is not an entity unto itself. It does not have the right to do what it wants or move the Charity in a direction that may not reflect the interests or the intentions of the Members.

If you have had any experience serving on a Board, I am inviting you to think in very different terms. Sometimes books on Board governance are nothing more than a clever reiteration of the same old ideas. What we are going to see in this chapter is very different.

A Whole New Game

In North America many people spend many weekends watching football. Football is played with an oblong ball on a field where the ball is thrown, caught (or dropped) and kicked; where players run, block, tackle and are tackled. This game is played in both Canada and the US, albeit with a few different nuances. In Canada there are three downs while in the U.S. there are four downs. The Canadian field is ten yards longer and about twelve yards wider. In the U.S. there are eleven players whereas in Canada there are twelve players on the field at one time. In Canada the defence scrimmages one-yard off the ball whereas in the U.S. it scrimmages on the line. These are just a few of a myriad of other minor variations. Nonetheless, American players come up to Canada all the time and play successfully on Canadian teams when they have never played on a Canadian field or by Canadian rules before. Why? Because football is football. Even within each league, rules are changed every year. But no matter how much the rules are changed, football will never evolve into baseball. Baseball is a different game, requiring an entirely different field, different equipment and different athletic skills.

As we begin to look at a new way of seeing how Boards can function, keep this analogy in mind. We are not tweaking the rules of the same game or making some minor adjustments to the playing field. This is a new game.

Policy Governance®

Around 1980, John Carver began to develop a model of Board leadership, which he termed Policy Governance. Governing with policies was neither a new concept nor one that was introduced by John Carver. However, the model of Policy Governance is a concept that he developed and is sometimes also referred to as the "Carver model." References to Policy Governance in this book are not to be taken as authoritative for interpreting or implementing the Policy Governance model. For a comprehensive understanding of Policy Governance, I recommend John Carver's books, such as *Boards That Make a Difference* and *Reinventing Your Board.*

At times, I am asked by various charities if there are other models of Board governance. I am quick to assure them that there is at least one other model… the one they are using now. It is crucial that you do not confuse Policy Governance with the ad hoc development of a variety of Board policies. Simply governing with policies is to the traditional way of Board governance, what Canadian football rules are to American football rules: the same game with a few different rules.

The restructuring of governance is invariably fuelled by a problem with the current model. The problem may be a Board that feels bogged down in detail it does not understand or senses its role is merely rubberstamping the initiatives of the Leader. Whatever the driving issue, incremental adjustments will only lead to incremental change and exponential frustration. The frustration is born out of the belief that nothing will ever really change.

Policy Governance is a helpful model in allowing Boards to govern and the Leader to manage the Charity. It will help to clear up the confusion and frustration discussed earlier. We are only going to take a look at the Policy Governance landscape from the 40,000-foot perspective but even from that height, you should be able to get a clear view of this governance model.

Let's start with the premise that the purpose of the Board is to govern. Any time the word *govern* is used, one must ask on whose behalf is the Board governing. For example, political governing bodies govern on behalf of the citizens of a particular country or community. For the purposes of this discussion, a Board governs on behalf of the Members of a Charity to make sure the objectives established by the Charity's founders, as confirmed in its incorporating documents and as supported by the Members, are indeed accomplished.

> The purpose of the Board is to govern. Any time the word *govern* is used, one must ask on whose behalf is the Board governing.

Traditional boards are typically faced with the responsibility to approve motions. Often the motion to approve is presented in such a way that withholding approval is not deemed appropriate; however, to be able to approve something assumes the opportunity and freedom to withhold approval. If you have sat on a Board when a motion has been presented for approval, try voting against the motion. I am not talking about some controversial issue on which there may be strongly held opinions, but just one of those mundane, innocuous motions.

Let's suppose the Board of a private Christian school is required to approve all teacher hires. The name of Sally Jones is presented to the school Board for approval. "All in favour please indicate so by the raising of your right hand… all opposed please indicate in the same manner." Try raising your hand in opposition. The Chair and the rest of the Directors will look at you as though you were just a little late raising your hand in support—that is, until you make it clear that you are not approving the motion. The question will invariably be, "Why *not* approve the hiring?" when in fact the better question is, "Why *approve* the hiring"? You know little or nothing about the candidate other than what you may have seen on her *curriculum vitae.* No one on the Board, never mind you yourself, has met her or checked any of her references. Nevertheless you are asked to approve her hiring.

Your colleagues may talk about the fact that she has been interviewed by the principal, the vice-principal and the department head, all of whom deem her to be fully qualified. If they think she is qualified, what are you supposed to be offering? Notice how the subject is being subtly changed from granting approval to the evaluative process. Ironically it was the Board that hired the Principal in whose judgment it apparently had great confidence. If Sally Jones is good enough for the Principal, she should be good enough for the Board. If Sally is not an acceptable candidate to the Board, that is more of a commentary on the Board than it is on either Sally or the Principal. This form of mechanical approval is what many Boards do. It is called rubberstamping.

Policy Governance operates on preapprovals based on established limitations, rather than reactive approvals based on persuasive arguments or gut feelings. In the case of hiring Sally, some established limitations have been developed regarding the process of hiring teachers. For example, the Board may have a limitation stating that the Principal will not hire anyone who does not have a minimum educational degree of a Bachelor of Education, has not been interviewed and approved by the Principal and has not been checked out against an abuse or criminal registry. As long as any limitations established by the Board are not violated, the hiring of the teacher is preapproved.

A motion to approve anything must be based on having clear, established criteria against which you can approve or oppose the motion. If that is not in place, the most persuasive argument will prevail.

A domestic example will illustrate my point. But before I do that, let me provide an explanation. I never go shopping with my wife for her clothes and seldom go shopping for my own without her. Whatever she buys for herself or for me is just fine.

> A motion to approve anything must be based on having clear, established criteria against which you can approve or oppose the motion.

Having said that, let's suppose Lorna comes home with a new dress and tries it on for my approval. I know the right answer is "Yes I approve," but bear with me. First of all, I want to check the criteria for granting or withholding approval. Is it based on the style of the dress or the need for an updated wardrobe or the colour or the cost? Suppose my approval is based on all four conditions: style, need, colour and cost. To grant or withhold approval means that the details of each condition would need to have been established—otherwise my approval or disapproval would be random and subjective. It would be unreasonable for her to go shopping without knowing specifically what style of dress she could purchase, how much she could spend, what colour it needed to be and whether or not she needed it. Having covered those bases, I can determine if her purchase meets with my approval.

In the same way, you need to begin by finding out whether there is an option to grant or withhold approval before looking at the conditions for approval. There is no point in granting approval if withholding approval is not an option. In Policy Governance, the Board deals with motions in a strategic, proactive and informed way rather than being pressured into approving motions without sufficient understanding or information.

ENDS

Policy Governance divides every issue into one of two categories. It is either an *Ends* issue or a *Means* issue.

> There is no point in granting approval if withholding approval is not an option.

Ends describe what benefit will result, specifically who will benefit and the cost/value of that benefit. "Sort of like a mission statement?" you ask. Later on we will be looking at mission statements and what they accomplish, but mission statements often describe why a Charity exists within the context of what the Charity does. Terms such as *create, develop, offer* or *provide* are often used in mission statements. The assumption in Policy Governance is that no Charity exists for what it *does*. A Charity exists so that certain people will be specifically better off and that it will be done at a reasonable cost. A private school, for example, may have an Ends policy stating that the school exists so that students will graduate with the qualifications necessary to pursue post-secondary education at a cost comparable to other private schools in the area. The beneficiary is the student, the benefit is an education that equips that student for post-secondary education and the cost is reasonable as determined by comparative tuitions with other private schools in the area.

The ongoing development of Ends policies and the monitoring of those policies should reflect much of the Board's work. These policies describe the long-term destination of the Charity, including the specific outcomes. These are the policies to which the Board must hold its Leader accountable. It is not the role of the Board to produce those results, but to ensure that they are produced by the Leader.

MEANS

The definition of *Means* in Policy Governance is very simple; anything that is not an End is a Means. While Ends define the benefits of the Charity in

> The assumption in Policy Governance is that no Charity exists for what it *does*.

terms of who is better off and how they are better off, Means define how the Charity will operate so that the benefits are being realized.

The Ends of *The Caring Kitchen* may be that undernourished people within a certain area will have access to a healthy meal on a regular basis. Renting a facility, making soup and cleaning up are all Means used to accomplish the prescribed Ends.

BACK TO THE BOARD

The Board's responsibility is to clearly know its role and to know whether it is performing its role.

The first role is to hear from the Members so the Board understands what the Members and the Moral Owners see as the benefits of the Charity. It is not up to the Board of *The Caring Kitchen* to decide if *The Caring Kitchen* is a soup kitchen or a teaching school for the culinary arts. It needs to be attentive to what its Members are saying.

Secondly, the Board needs to make certain that the Ends are accomplished. This is done by delegating the accomplishment of the Ends to the Leader in the form of carefully written policies. Finally, once those Ends policies have been developed, the Board needs to monitor the Leader to make sure the Ends are being realized.

The Board does not concern itself with the day-to-day Means to realizing Ends. Does that mean the Leader has the unilateral right to use any Means they want? The answer is "Almost yes." The Leader can use any Means they want, *except* those Means which are prohibited by the Board. The example of the private school can illustrate this. While the Board wants to ensure students receive a quality education, the Leader, the principal, is not entitled to use any Means at hand to accomplish that End. The principal cannot cut financial corners by underpaying teachers or having the school understaffed or in disrepair. Even if cutting corners reduces costs and decreasing tuition raises enrolment so more students are benefited, these Means are still unacceptable. The Board will typically express these limitations by using proscriptive or negative language. In other words, the Board will not typically state what Means the Leader *can* use but rather what Means *cannot* be used. For example, "The principal *shall not* permit a classroom to have more than twenty-five students."

Some observers of Policy Governance see the idea of limitations being expressed in negative language as being—well—negative. In this case, though, negative is really positive. If limitations were expressed in terms of what is permitted, the assumption would be that anything that is not permitted is prohibited. "Unless we tell you it is permissible, it's not." Policy Governance on the other hand starts with the assumption that everything is permitted and then goes on to state the exceptions.

Summary

I began this chapter by decrying the bombardment of a Board with excessive operational and managerial detail that it cannot possibly absorb. Furthermore, we saw that the Board is not fulfilling its fiduciary responsibility by making decisions about which it does not have a complete understanding quite apart from an appreciation of the implications.

We have concluded that a Board exists to govern on behalf of its Members by ensuring the Charity is accomplishing the purposes for which it exists, while at the same time making sure that no prohibited Means are used in accomplishing those purposes.

In the next chapter we are going to address the question as to how a Board can measure what is being accomplished. Once it has answered that question, the next obvious question is whether or not what is supposed to be accomplished is being accomplished.

?

How Does a Charity Define Success?

The Importance of Measuring the Right Results

WHAT'S THE BOTTOM LINE?

That's the question asked by owners when wanting to determine the success of their business. There can be pages of information about income and expenses, year-to-date comparisons and actual to budget. However, in the end it comes down to whether the company made money for the owner(s) and if it made enough money to warrant the effort and the risk.

Any company that manufactures goods or provides a service assumes there is a market for those goods or services. The company believes that if an individual buys a furnace or enlists their company to sell a home, the customer will receive a benefit worth the cost that was paid for that benefit. When that happens, former customers return and recommendations are made to potential customers.

When the Bottom Line is Not Easy to See

For a Charity, identifying the bottom line can be somewhat more challenging. At the same time, there are many similarities. Potential beneficiaries in a business are referred to as customers who will receive some clear and quantifiable benefit. A Charity also provides a benefit to an identifiable group of beneficiaries.

But what about the bottom line? We have seen that a Charity does not exist to generate a financial profit or pay out financial dividends to its "shareholders," known as Members. Remember, we found out by understanding ownership in the context of a Charity that a Charity by definition cannot have shareholders.

How, then, does it define success?

First there must be some kind of benefit. It may be warm housing or good education or nutritious food. The housing, education and food must have an identifiable beneficiary: warm housing for the homeless, quality education for the students or nutritious food for the hungry. Secondly, there is the cost benefit. A benefit may be provided to the beneficiary, but at a cost that is not justifiable. How many homeless people are housed, how many meals are eaten or how many students are being educated and at what cost? Is the cost for those benefits on a per-person basis an amount that can be considered reasonable? There is little point in having a homeless shelter if someone could be housed in a hotel for the same amount. Why set up a Charity to provide meals if individuals could be fed at a restaurant for the same amount or less? It may be noble to start a private school, but what if another private school is providing similar education at significantly less cost? The proposal for an additional private school would need to be carefully reconsidered.

The Challenge of Measuring Ends

In the previous chapter we talked briefly about Policy Governance being a new game and introducing Ends as a part that game. Ends are not something that flow naturally into the conversations or deliberations of a Board. In the Policy Governance model, the Board has a responsibility to develop Ends to make sure the objectives established by the Charity's founders, as confirmed in its incorporating documents, and as supported by the Members, are indeed accomplished. However, it is pointless to develop Ends policies if those policies are not monitored. Furthermore it is futile to monitor Ends if there are no criteria against which the achievement of those Ends can be evaluated and measured.

Christian charities and particularly churches sometimes have a perspective which is somewhat mystical and potentially subjective. And while there is an element of reality to that perspective, a church should not be satisfied just to have increased attendance, effective programs and balanced budgets. More precisely, a church should not even exist for those reasons alone. If a church exists so people will be *better Christians*, how can that possibly be quantified in a way that will demonstrate the Ends are being achieved?

It May Be Challenging But it is Vital

There is the school of thought that espouses that "people are important, not numbers," as though they are mutually exclusive. The graduates of such a school obviously miss one of the basic teachings of Jesus in the New Testament. He spoke of the need to invest resources wisely and to see a return on the investment of those resources. If the resources of time, people, energy and money are invested, some quantifiable way of measuring the return on those investments is needed. If that is not done, not only will the Charity have no way of knowing whether or not the desired Ends are achieved, there is no way of knowing if the resources could be invested differently and more effectively.

Suppose a business spends $10,000 on advertising and was able to prove the advertising investment yielded an $11,000 gross income. One could argue that the $10,000 was well spent because it resulted in a $1,000 profit that would not have been otherwise realized. However, if that same $10,000 could have been spent differently, resulting in $12,000 gross income, then the business in effect just lost $1,000 profit.

Using the same analogy, if by spending $10, one person was benefited in a quantifiable way, it could be argued that the $10 was well spent. However, if by spending that $10 differently, two people were equally benefited instead of one, then it follows that the original investment of $10 resulted in the loss of one person being benefited.

If you are a Director of a Christian Charity you know that spiritual progress cannot be objectively quantified in the way I have suggested. The issue is not whether the resour-

ces have accomplished something, but whether those same
resources could have been better used. If no efforts are ever
made to evaluate the benefits
of a Charity, there is no way to
evaluate its effectiveness. How

> If no efforts are ever made to evaluate the benefits of a Charity, there is no way to evaluate its effectiveness.

can a Charity know whether or not it is succeeding? Is it possible to know if what is being done is producing the expected
or hoped for results? If the work of the Charity is all about
people and not about numbers, then arguably one person
per evening eating at a soup kitchen is acceptable regardless
of the cost. Should a Charity attempt to evaluate its ministry
success or just keep doggedly plodding on? And when has
the Charity done enough plodding?

INCREMENTAL PROGRESS AS A MEASURE OF SUCCESS

Suppose I want to lose weight—and I do! How will I know if
I have succeeded? If I lose one pound, is that success? If I lose
five pounds, do I see that as failure? Losing a pound or five
pounds cannot be defined as either success or failure, unless I
start out by knowing (a) how much weight I want to lose and
(b) the timeframe within which I want to lose that weight.

Let's assume my goal is to lose twenty pounds in twenty
weeks. If I lose nineteen pounds in one week does that constitute success? No, not if my goal is to lose twenty pounds. If I
lose one pound in nineteen weeks is that necessarily failure?
No, not if I still have one more week in which to reach my
goal of losing twenty pounds. Thus a third requirement for

determining success is needed. I need to have established incremental measurements of progress or improvement. I may want to set a goal of losing two pounds per week for the first three weeks and a pound per week for the next few weeks and finish off by losing half a pound a week.

Success is determined by continual improvement or progress (losing weight) measured by the established metrics of how much weight I want to lose over a given period of time and at a given rate. Simple enough isn't it?

Metrics Don't Prove Anything

> Success is determined by continual improvement or progress... measured by the established metrics

I know all too well from personal experience that it is not that simple. I was told that if I bought a membership to a gym that I would lose weight. So I tried that but it didn't help. Then I found out I actually have to *go* to the gym. Furthermore, it's not just a matter of getting inside the doors. I actually need to use some of the equipment. I have to intentionally deal with the amount of weight lifted, calories burned and heart rate reached.

So why am I doing all this? (A question I ask every time I make my way to the gym.) I will want to look more deeply at *why* I wanted to lose weight. My doctor told me that losing weight would decrease the likelihood of a stroke, a heart attack or diabetes. Knowing I don't want to experience any of the three, I am willing to go through the regimen of working out at the gym and having healthy eating habits.

Do I know if losing twenty pounds in twenty weeks guarantees I will not have a heart attack? Or what if I don't lose any weight; am I guaranteed to have a heart attack? The answer to both those questions of course is "no." So going through the agony of losing weight doesn't prove that I won't have a heart attack nor does a sedentary lifestyle guarantee that I will have a stroke.

WHY BOTHER WITH METRICS?

Back to my original question: Why am I doing all this? Why did I decide to lose twenty pounds and not ten or fifteen pounds? My decision to lose twenty pounds is based on advice and medical information that extra weight and extra fat increases the likelihood of a heart attack. My decision will be further confirmed by surveys which demonstrate that people who have 30% body fat are more likely to have a heart attack than those who have only 20% body fat.

My answer begins with my ultimate goal: that of responsibility to my family to keep myself healthy. Naturally I want to have a healthy body

> Develop a plan which is identifiable, measurable and achievable.

that allows me to enjoy life, enjoy my family, my health and my job. Having embraced the conviction that losing weight will increase the likelihood of reaching my goal of being there for my family, I must develop a plan which is identifiable, measurable and achievable. In so doing, I have no guarantee my ultimate goal will be reached.

> Failure is not necessarily the opposite of success. Success is a journey, not a destination.

Failure is not necessarily the opposite of success. Success is a journey, not a destination.

What does this have to do with the work of a Charity? Back to our original question: How do we *know* that what the Charity is doing is producing the results the Members want to see? Like the weight loss analogy, we are presented with a conundrum. On one hand we are dealing with numbers: pounds, inches, weeks, calories and heart beats per minute. On the other hand we acknowledge that any amount of exercising won't guarantee a healthy heart, nor does inactivity mean a heart attack is inevitable.

A Board faces the same challenge. It can be preoccupied with meals served, students graduated, and attendance trends while losing sight of the purpose for which the Charity exists. Conversely if a Board concedes it is all about people and not about Ends statements, does it have no responsibility for discerning whether the Ends are being achieved or the wishes of the Members are being realized? Boards often equate hard work with success, assuming

> Boards often equate hard work with success, assuming there is a direct correlation between activity and productivity.

there is a direct correlation between activity and productivity. On the other hand, Boards can adopt the hyper-spiritual *God has not called us to be successful, just faithful; so let's work hard and leave the results with Him* attitude. We must avoid the temptation of either extreme. One end of the spectrum can leave us with a passive resignation that we cannot or should not measure success. The other end has us obsessively preoccupied with numbers that in themselves prove nothing.

So how do we strike a balance?

A Personal Evaluation

This exercise has challenged me to ask myself how *Ted Hull Consulting* is doing. Income is one readily identifiable measurement. However, there are other measurements, including the number of counselling sessions, the number of clients, the number of consulting contracts and of course the number of books sold.

When Measuring Success Is Elusive

Over the years as a counsellor I have been asked about my success rate. Success as a counsellor is virtually impossible to quantify with any degree of objectivity. For example, a woman comes for counselling and tells me she has been beaten by her husband and has moved out. Suppose I counsel her to go back to her husband, be a better wife and he will change. (No, I have never offered this advice!) If one of my metrics is couples who were separated and are now back together, my "success" rate would increase based on the number of reunited couples, regardless of the quality of their life together or the process by which they reunited.

Success in those terms is measured using an inaccurate metric. I should do what is in the best interests of my client, rather than being driven by an ill-conceived metric. In one situation, that may mean encouraging a husband to leave his mistress and go back to his wife and children. In another situation it may involve counsel that urges a woman to remove herself from an abusive relationship.

Charities must avoid the subtle temptation of using criteria to measure success just for the sake of the measurement. Here are some suggestions for ways that a Charity can quantify the achievement of its Ends.

Raw Numbers

Numbers are the easiest and most obvious way to measure success—the low-hanging fruit if you will. Numbers can include meals served, students graduating or people attending church services. You begin with a base line or bench mark and then look for "an increase" or "add more" along with a timeline for reaching those goals. In doing so, you must state the level of increase or how many more. Failure to define these terms provides wiggle room as well as excuses for minimal advancements. Remember my weight-loss plan? The good news is I lost 20 pounds. The bad news is that I am losing the same pounds over and over again. When comparing numbers, you want to start and end with the same scale. If I am going to measure my weight loss, I need to use the same scale and the same baseline. I shouldn't weigh myself now with my cell phone on my belt and a pocket full of change and then weigh myself a month later without the added weight. Make sure that when you are setting the metrics, there is no room for manipulating the numbers.

It is important that the numbers used are comprehensive and reflective of the Ends policies. An example of this would be our friends at *The Caring Kitchen*. Suppose one of the Ends of *The Caring Kitchen* is that homeless people will have access to a safe place where they can have a nutritious meal. Serving more meals (which is a Means and not an End) in itself is not a measure of success, if it includes allowing people under the influence of drugs or alcohol to have a meal. That would be like me weighing myself with my hand on the table. The scale may show I weigh less, but it doesn't tell me if I am actually healthier. If there is a comparison of apples to apples, having more people eating healthier meals can be easily quantified.

OPPORTUNITIES

Another Ends policy for *The Caring Kitchen* may sound like this: "Because of *The Caring Kitchen*, members of the local community will have the opportunity to make a difference in the lives of those less fortunate." This assumes that volunteer involvement is an End. If volunteers are a Means to accomplishing the End of homeless people having access to a safe place where they can have a nutritious meal, then it should not be used. "Make a difference" can be subjective and difficult to quantify. However, we can measure the environment for those opportunities. If *The Caring Kitchen* wants people to have the experience of interacting with the less fortunate, the opportunities for people to access that experience can be measured. How many volunteers are involved? For how long do they continue to be involved? What is the satisfaction rate as measured by the desired outcome? Measure volunteer satisfaction against a standard that is consistent with your Ends. People may not have a positive experience because the patrons are dirty or messy, or worse because "they are not like me," but that is not a good measurement of volunteer satisfaction.

Surveys

Surveys allow you to receive feedback anonymously. This measurement tool needs to be used carefully and is not applicable to every situation or every Charity. Using a survey to measure Volunteer satisfaction is useful but it may be less practical for measuring the impact on the guests of *The Caring Kitchen*.

Surveys need to be developed carefully. Make sure the questions will result in useful information. Surveys can be a good example of *garbage in — garbage out*. For example, asking people if they would be willing to serve more if they were paid is pointless if you have no intention of paying them. Those surveyed may interpret the question as something the Charity is considering when in fact, it is just an empty question.

Demographic questions will provide important information. For example, are younger Volunteers more satisfied than older Volunteers? Are females more likely to feel more compassionate as a result of their volunteer experience?

A survey can be helpful in setting baselines for future measurements. If the satisfaction rate for a survey question such as experiencing greater or lesser compassion results in 25% of Volunteers feeling less compassionate or more disillusioned after serving for a given period of time, you have a benchmark. After one survey, you won't know what is "normal." Provide some more teaching on why people are homeless and the mental challenges that exacerbate homelessness. Follow this up with another survey and you could rightfully anticipate an increase in the level of compassion. Surveys are exponentially more valuable when they are repeated using the same criteria and the same questions which is why it is very important to get the questions right the first time.

ANECDOTES

Anecdotal evidence as data is less objective than raw numbers, but evaluation of such evidence in the context of Ends can provide creative and helpful ways of measuring success. Admittedly, an anecdote can be the isolated experience of one person who tells you a story that is consistent with what you want to hear. At the same time, stories about people's lives that have been radically changed by the ministry of the Charity are powerful and affirming.

Suppose you hear a story of an indigent woman whose life was powerfully impacted by the kindness of a volunteer at *The Caring Kitchen*. She has made some significant changes to her lifestyle due in part to the kindness and care she received because someone took a special interest in her. Or how about a story of a volunteer who signed up because they felt pressured by a friend, but who gained a new appreciation for people, disenfranchised by circumstances over which they had no control. The Volunteer talks about how their attitude toward these people has shifted from a pragmatic, "get-a-job" attitude toward one of compassion and concern for the less fortunate.

Obviously, a couple of poignant stories do not justify the Ends of a Charity. Limited use of the soup kitchen, unfulfilling opportunities to serve and survey results that trend in a negative direction cannot be negated by a heart-warming story or two. Nonetheless, the impact of increasing numbers, engaged volunteers and positive surveys can be underscored by touching life stories.

"Ah, yes," you say, "But how can that be quantifiably measured?" While the impact of each story itself cannot be measured, it is helpful to keep track of the stories to demonstrate the cumulative impact of the Charity. A newsletter may contain one of these stories each month. If the Charity is hard-pressed to come up with one story a month, that metric should be cause for concern. Look for genuine stories that reflect your stated Ends.

So What Have We Proven?

Do these methods of measuring success prove anything? As I mentioned earlier, I have been forced to ask myself if my services are successful. To do that, I need to have certain criteria against which success is measured.

Appropriate numbers are one indicator that the Ends of *Ted Hull Consulting* are being realized. However, I need to look at other, less objective measurements.

Unedited feedback from clients is invaluable. It is easy to write off my critics, accepting only the responses I want to hear. All opinions need to be evaluated against my Ends. Are charities empowered to move from where they are to where they want to be? Are counselling clients now asking more

> My desire for determining progress and success *must* be intrinsic. I *have* to want to know; I have to *need* to know.

informed questions about their situation? You can see my penchant for having individuals asking informed questions that move them in a good direction.

I can measure my personal development with some degree of objectivity. One way is by tracking how many books I have read on the subjects of governance, leadership and relationships. In the same way that losing weight does not guarantee I will not have a heart attack, reading good books does not prove I am a better consultant as a result of reading certain books. It will not directly translate into more business, more positive testimonials or more referrals. Nevertheless, based on my assumption that I will be a better consultant if I read more good books, I will set a metric of reading a certain number of books or pages over a certain period of time.

My desire for determining progress and success *must* be intrinsic. I *have* to want to know; I have to *need* to know. I will want to speak with others involved in the same kind of work

> Measuring results is risky.

I am doing. I may get some good ideas relating to the measurement of success. These ideas are less about *how* I measure and more about *why* I measure. If I am not ruthlessly examining the advancement and success of my services, I will never know if I'm moving forward. Tragically, I will also never know if I'm moving backwards.

Measuring results is risky. Measuring my investment and my exposure against measured returns may expose some weaknesses or shortcomings. Failing to measure results does not change them. It only keeps me uninformed and unaccountable.

Charities must be diligent in the ongoing evaluation of their Ends. They owe it to their Members as well as those whom they are seeking to benefit.

Summary

We have examined the need to be conscientious about measuring success as well as some ideas how that can be accomplished. Hopefully you have seen success as being less about a one-time goal to be reached and more about reaching incremental markers indicating movement in the right direction. If a Charity is moving in the wrong direction, this should provide an opportunity for reflection and redirection. When progress is achieved, measuring success provides a great opportunity to celebrate.

?

Question #8

How Does a Board Insure the Ends Don't Justify Any Means?

Limitations — Any Means Will Do, Except…

HOPEFULLY YOU HAVE LEARNED AT LEAST two things about governing a Charity. The first is when anything goes wrong it is a failure of the Board to govern well. The second is that a Board must not micromanage. Or as Jim Brown says in his book, *The Imperfect Board Member,* "The best boards keep their noses in the business and their fingers out!" (Brown 88)

The Caring Kitchen has hired a Leader to oversee the operational implementation of the Ends that have been set by the Board; however, the Board must not allow any and all Means to be used to meet those Ends. In this chapter we are going to look at *Executive Limitations,* which is the term used in Policy Governance to describe those policies which limit the Means that can be used by the Leader. By using Executive Limitation

> When anything goes wrong it is a failure of the Board to govern well.

policies, the Board implicitly tells the Leader that any Means can be used to realize the Ends set out by the Board, while explicitly stating those Means which are prohibited by the Board. These prohibited Means may even include Means that save money or increase operational efficiencies.

Negative is Positive

Executive Limitations are usually written in the negative. Rather than stating what a Leader *can* do, Executive Limitations are crafted on the assumption that the Leader can use any Means except those prohibited. As well, they are written from a broad or global perspective moving toward an increasing level of specificity. Once the Board has reached a level of specificity or detail after which it is willing to accept *any reasonable interpretation*, it can stop.

Stating Executive Limitations in the negative is positive. What some boards see as positive, "permission-granting" language, by default implies that permission is withheld—that a Leader cannot do anything unless permission is granted. Conversely in Policy Governance, negative, "permission-limiting" language defaults to permission being granted to the Leader to use any Means with only the exceptions being stated. Expressing Executive Limitations in this manner gives greater freedom to the Leader and makes the Board's work less onerous.

The following admittedly unrelated example cast in Policy Governance language illustrates the value of Executive Limitations.

Suppose I give my Executive Assistant the responsibility for ensuring there are refreshments for an upcoming meeting. My *Refreshment Policy* might say, "The Executive Assistant shall not fail to provide refreshments for the upcoming meeting." If this requires more than a simple request I have other problems, but stick with me. While this limitation is very general, I must ask myself if I am willing to accept *any reasonable interpretation* of the policy.

What might an *unreasonable interpretation* look like? Surely it would not be reasonable to have a dozen shot glasses of coffee or have the coffee delivered in a five-gallon pail. Can we further agree that it would not be a reasonable interpretation to have coffee provided without cream and sugar?

Based on my *Refreshment Policy*, my Executive Assistant could reasonably interpret that coffee and donuts would constitute compliance. Am I willing to accept *any reasonable interpretation* of that policy? Am I willing to accept caffeinated coffee and high-carb donuts as a reasonable interpretation of the *Refreshments Policy*? If so, there is no need for me to be more specific. If that is not acceptable, then it is up to me to provide greater specificity about what is prohibited. The policy could be written as:

> 1.0 The Executive Assistant shall not fail to provide refreshments at the upcoming meeting.

Under that policy there would be an additional policy such as:

> 1.1 The Executive Assistant shall not fail to
> provide a variety of hot and cold beverages
> and healthy snacks.

Now let's see if I am willing to accept any reasonable interpretation of that policy. If my Executive Assistant provides coffee, tea, bottled water and a veggie plate, would that be acceptable? Keep in mind that I have not specified whether the coffee is decaf or if there is herbal tea or if cold beverages include pop and bottled water or if there are vegetables other than broccoli and cauliflower. If I am willing to accept *any reasonable interpretation* of that policy, then I can stop there. If I want more restrictions, then those need to be stated.

Now let's move to an example of an Executive Limitation. Most Executive Limitations will start with a global policy such as:

> 1.0 The Leader shall not cause or allow any or-
> ganizational practice, activity, decision or cir-
> cumstance that is unlawful, imprudent or in
> violation of commonly accepted business and
> professional ethics and practices.

A church or Christian Charity may add "scriptural" to this global policy.

Clearly such a global policy covers off virtually everything for which a Leader could be responsible. With such a comprehensive, but high-level policy, the Board will likely want to add more specificity.

Our general or global policy includes not causing or allowing anything that is imprudent or unwise. It would seem apparent that to allow the capital assets of a Charity to be uninsured or the data files not to be backed up would be imprudent. A Board usually prefers the issue of asset protection to be more specific, which leads to the next level:

> 2.0 The Leader shall not allow any of the organization's assets to be unnecessarily exposed to risk.

Given policy 2.0, the Board must consider if it is willing to accept *any reasonable interpretation* of that policy. Will the Leader be in compliance with the policy by purchasing some insurance or making sure the data files are backed up every week or two? Suppose such action was deemed by the Leader to be a reasonable interpretation but was not deemed satisfactory to the Board. The Board has the ultimate responsibility to ensure the assets of the Charity are protected. Therefore as it relates to the loss of physical assets, the Board will add another level stating that:

> 3.0 The Leader shall not fail to adequately insure the assets of the Charity against theft, loss or damage.

This policy addresses not only the need for insurance but the need for the insurance to provide adequate coverage. If this is acceptable, the Board does not need to go any further. In some cases the Board may want to add a further limitation by ensuring that the Leader insures capital assets for not less than a certain percentage of their replacement value. Note that the Board has not provided a limitation on the number of quotes the Leader must receive. That is covered in the more general policy of not allowing for anything imprudent (i.e. accepting the first quote), without going into the detail of obtaining quotes. Having chosen not to add this limitation, the Board cannot evaluate the performance of the Leader based on how many quotes were received. If the assets of the Charity suffer theft, loss or damage, the Board may want to blame the Leader; but it is the ultimate responsibility of the Board to make sure that the Leader does not fail to procure sufficient insurance.

Think of a Board with which you may be currently associated. Do you know if the Charity is sufficiently insured? A better question might be whether you have any idea what *sufficient coverage* would even be.

> Everything that takes place or fails to take place within a Charity is the ultimate responsibility of the Board.

Remember that everything that takes place or fails to take place within a Charity is the ultimate responsibility of the Board. This includes everything from permitting conditions that would allow for child abuse in a church nursery to a failure to have sufficient paperclips in the office of a social agency. No doubt you will readily agree with the former but you may have problems with the latter. How can a Board possibly get into the details of making sure there are enough paperclips in the office supply cupboard? The answer to that question is the same as "How can a Board ensure children are not abused in a nursery?" In both cases it delegates. Delegation is trading authority for accountability. The Board may have an Executive Limitation policy such as:

4.0 The Leader will not fail to have procedures in place that minimize the possibility of harm being perpetrated against children by child care workers, other children or other persons who may have authorized or unauthorized access to children.

The Leader will in turn delegate the implementation of that policy to a volunteer or employee, but the Board will look only to the Leader for an assurance of compliance.

> Delegation is trading authority for accountability.

How about paperclips? On one hand this has been covered by the global policy that we referred to at the beginning of the chapter, by which the Leader will not allow a practice that is in violation of generally accepted business practices. This is an example of the Board not being any more specific than the level of detail in the global policy. The Board could have a more specific policy by which the Leader must not allow the staff to operate without the necessary resources. In this case, paperclips are assumed to be a necessary resource. I am not encouraging a Board to have an Executive Limitation regarding paperclips or even office supplies. If it has to get into that degree of specificity with the Leader, you likely have other, more serious problems. The paperclip issue should be covered by *any reasonable interpretation* of the existing policies. The Board should not develop more specific Executive Limitation policies unless it is unwilling to accept any reasonable interpretation of the more general policy.

The interpretation of a policy is always the interpretation given by the Leader as they understand the policy. Hence it is very important for the Board to clearly articulate the policy and choose its words carefully. A policy is not a legal document. Legal documents can sometimes (read: always) be intentionally ambiguous—providing loopholes for the party writing them. Executive Limitation policies are written to clearly communicate the intention of the Board. The interpretation given by the Leader serves to show that both the Leader and the Board have the same understanding of the policy. If the policy is written in such a way that the intention of the Board and the interpretation of the Leader are different, the Board needs to edit the policy. This assumes that the Leader has *reasonably* interpreted the policy.

Don't Treat These Policies Like Most Policies

You know what happens to most policies. They are carefully worded, placed in exquisite binders… and ignored; that is, until something goes wrong. Then it is pulled off the shelf, dusted off and used to beat the offender over the head (figuratively of course).

Monitor, Monitor, Monitor

Delegation is the exchange of authority—having the Charity properly insured—for accountability—having the Leader demonstrate that the Charity is properly insured. If the Board is going to delegate its authority, it must have a way to clearly and regularly monitor compliance with the delegated authority. It is not good enough to tell a Leader that the

Ends of the Charity can be pursued using any Means except the ones which are prohibited if compliance with those prohibitions is not monitored. I cannot emphasize strongly enough that monitoring must be consistent with the policies. Do not

> If the Board is going to delegate its authority, it must have a way to clearly and regularly monitor compliance with the delegated authority.

have Executive Limitation policies you are not prepared to monitor, and do not monitor expectations which have not been stated. The Board must not surrender authority without receiving accountability that confirms compliance. Delegation without accountability is irresponsible on the part of the Board. Accountability without delegation renders the Leader irrelevant.

Referring to the Asset Protection policy:

> 3.0 The Leader shall not fail to adequately insure the assets of the Charity against theft, loss or damage.

> Do not have Executive Limitation policies you are not prepared to monitor, and do not monitor expectations which have not been stated.

The Leader may interpret "adequately" as "sufficiently ensuring that all physical property including building and contents are insured in an amount not less than the appraised value as determined by the insurer." In so doing, the Leader is interpreting the Board's understanding of "adequate." The Board will need to decide if it accepts that as a

reasonable interpretation. Assuming acceptance of that interpretation, the Leader will state whether they are in compliance with that policy. If the Leader is not in compliance, the
Board will see this noted in the Monitoring Report with an
explanation of the non-compliance and what will be done to
move back into compliance.

VARIOUS WAYS OF MONITORING

> Delegation without
> accountability is
> irresponsible on the
> part of the Board.
> Accountability without
> delegation renders the
> Leader irrelevant.

The Board has the prerogative
to audit compliance by whatever means it chooses. The
most important way is through
the regular Monitoring Report.
If the Board failed to follow up
to see if the Leader was operating within the asset protec-
tion limitation, it would be at the very least embarrassing,
and potentially disastrous. It remains the responsibility of
the Board to ensure the Charity is adequately insured and
to clearly mandate the Leader to obtain sufficient coverage.
Having done so, it is then the Board's responsibility to monitor compliance with the requirement that the Leader purchase adequate insurance.

If the Asset Protection policy includes a limitation that
does not allow the Leader to insure for less than 80% of the
replacement value, then compliance to that limitation is required and must be monitored. However, if the Board decides not to include this limitation, then the Leader cannot
be monitored on an expectation that has not been stated by

the Board. If the Board is not willing to accept any reasonable interpretation of the most specific level of an Executive Limitation policy, then it must be more specific. If it wants insurance to cover no less than 80% of the replacement value, then it must be stated it in the policy.

Executive Limitations must be clearly stated and regularly monitored. The Board can monitor as frequently as it wants, but minimally at least once a year. The Leader must be duly advised when a monitoring report is due.

A Monitoring Report consists of four parts:

1. The policy.

2. The Leader's interpretation of the policy. In the case of the Asset Protection policy, terms such as "adequate coverage" or "regular backup" may have been used. The Leader may interpret "adequate coverage" by using 80% as their definition of "adequate." "Regular backup" may be defined by the Leader as being daily. The Board will decide if it is willing to accept this as a reasonable interpretation after receiving the report.

3. The supporting data to demonstrate compliance.

4. The declaration of compliance or non-compliance. In the case of non-compliance, the Leader will explain why they are not in compliance and what will be done to

move back into compliance. The Monitoring Report is then sent to the Board prior
to the next Board meeting.

Summary

In this chapter we have seen that the Ends do not justify any
Means. The Board must clearly state which Means are not
acceptable, even if the Ends could be achieved through those
prohibited Means. We have looked at a sample policy and
determined that the policy will only be as detailed as necessary so the Board can accept any reasonable interpretation
the Leader will place on that policy. Finally, we saw that it is
vital that the Executive Limitation policies be monitored for
specific compliance and done on a regular basis.

In the next two chapters we will look specifically at the
two areas that elicit the biggest questions for a Board: how it
gets a handle on the staffing needs of the Leader and how it
deals with the budget.

?

Question #9

How Does a Board Respond to Requests for More Staff?

Proactive Limitations Versus Reactive Considerations

"I need more staff if this Charity is to move forward."

"I can't hire new employees or keep the employees I have if I don't pay them a reasonable wage."

"Our staff is overworked and burning out. I need more employees just to stay on top of all that we have to do now."

You won't attend many Board meetings before this dilemma shows up on the agenda. If a Board turns down a compelling argument from the Leader for more staff, the Board will be perceived as either heartless and uncaring or regressive and status quo. Avoiding those perceptions forces the Board to grit its governance teeth and authorize the hiring of more staff or grant significant salary increases to the current staff. Of course the Leader is not asking for a personal raise, but if raises are given to everyone else and not the Leader, the Board may fear being seen as unappreciative of the work of the Leader.

And in case you think this is a one-off problem—it isn't. Next year the same issue will come to the Board table.

What does a Board do?

In the previous chapter I introduced Executive Limitations as a part of Policy Governance. We saw the benefits of setting proactive, clearly stated limitations. Now let's see how that works with the seemingly endless need for more staff or more money for current staff.

Remember that Executive Limitations are just that—limitations. They allow the Leader to use any Means except those which are prohibited. The Board needs to ask itself what Means it will not accept and specifically in this case as it relates to the amount of money that should be spent on salaries.

First, look at the total employee costs incurred by the Charity, including all employer costs such as CPP, EI and employee benefit plans. Also determine the cost of all contracted services except those that are exempt. The Board may exempt independent audit fees because an auditor cannot be an employee of the Charity. The Board may also want to exempt legal fees, as a Charity does not typically have legal counsel as part of its staff. It may want to exempt website designers from inclusion in the calculation of employee costs. In the end, the Board knows the current cost of employees and contractors.

Second, the Board will want to establish a benchmark for the percentage of the budget designated for employee costs. Difficult as it is, this process needs to be undertaken. The current employee costs are dependent on the number of employees and the salary earned by each of them. That may sound like a profound statement of the obvious, but there are two questions for which the Board must have answers.

First: Does the Charity have sufficient qualified staff? An assessment needs to be made regarding the current staffing requirements. At the very least, this will include a detailed discussion with the Leader. It may require an outside assessment of the staffing needs and whether those needs are being reached or exceeded. In a smaller Charity that will be less of a challenge. In a larger Charity, a third-party assessment may need to be done department by department. Eventually the Board must land on a recommendation that is amenable to the Leader and which will serve as a baseline for the number of employees needed under the current operating scenario. Even if the Board concedes a number that is marginally higher than it would have preferred, it serves as a baseline. It can happen that a Charity is overstaffed because it has taken on ministries that are outside its mandate. That issue, however, falls beyond the scope of this chapter.

A second question: Is the required staffing contingent being paid commensurate with employees in similar charities in the same geographical area? In 2007 the Canadian Council of Christian Charities conducted a comprehensive survey showing the salary range and benefits of a range of staff positions in various parts of the country among a variety of charities. The results of this survey can assist a Charity in developing some benchmarks for salaries among their employees.

The answers to these two questions will give the Board a good idea of how many employees are needed and the salary range for each category of employee. That combined number, along with contract costs, represents a percentage of the total budget of the Charity. The percentage of the budget spent on salaries will have a wide range, depending in part on the type of Charity.

Suppose the percentage of the budget designated to salaries is 50%. The impact of a new hiring is much greater if that percentage represents three employees as compared to thirty employees. If the Charity with three employees hires one new employee, that will drastically affect the percentage of the budget devoted to salaries. Conversely if the Charity loses an employee, the percentage will drop significantly. As a consequence of setting this limitation, the Board may need to consider a rolling average percentage over a three- or five-year period when determining the percentage of the budget spent on salaries.

Once a Board has settled on a baseline, it can develop an Executive Limitation policy. This policy could be:

> 1.0 The Leader shall not allow the cost for employees, including the employer costs of CPP, EI contributions and employee benefits as well as all contractors, with the exception of independent audit costs and legal costs, to exceed an average of 50% based on a five-year rolling average.

The Leader then will have an interpretation of that policy, present it to the Board and allow the Board to decide if it deems the interpretation to be reasonable. The Board will likely want to include a second policy to ensure that employees are paid a fair salary.

This results in two limitations related to staffing costs for the Leader. The first is the percentage of the budget that can be spent on salaries. The second is the limitation that does not allow employees to be underpaid or overpaid.

If you are a Leader wondering if this will be beneficial going forward, I'll let you in on a secret. Assuming you are a good Leader and the ministry grows, there will be some efficiency in economies of scale. Twice as much income will not require twice as many managers, administrative assistants or cleaning staff. The cost of salaries will increase, but not at the same rate as the income.

If as a Director you see this as a challenge at the front end, you are correct; but be assured—the long-term savings in time and hassle will be well worth the initial energy spent. Once the benchmarks have been established, the policies have been developed and the interpretations have been made, the Board only needs to monitor whether the Leader is compliant with those policies. No longer does the Board concern itself with whether a new employee can be hired or if an employee should receive a $1,000 per year salary increase. At the same time this gives the Leader flexibility relating to salaries as well as creating new positions as the Charity grows.

In governing under the Policy Governance model, the Board develops limitations that are proactive—dealing with issues on the basis of established policies. This puts an end to a Board having to make decisions on an ad hoc or reactive basis.

SUMMARY

We have seen how an Executive Limitations policy empowers the Leader to budget for staffing and salaries. At the same time it frees the Board from dealing with the hiring of new employees, setting salaries (except for that of the Leader) and the decisions that must then be made around that responsibility. The Board has set limitations in this area and freed itself from the need to micromanage staffing details.

In the next chapter we are going to look at one more area that typically eats up so much of the Board's time, and see how Policy Governance allows the Board to assume its responsibility without micromanaging, rubberstamping or even tweaking.

We will look at the budget.

?

Question #10

How Much Detail is Too Much in a Budget?

Decisions about Budgets

IF YOU HAVE EVER BEEN THE PARENT OF A teen with a driver's license or recall your days as a teen yourself, you can relate to the following scenario.

"Can I borrow the car?" Note: only ask that question if the parent is in a good mood.

"Where are you going?"

"To visit a friend."

"Which friend?" Note: this assumes a preapproved list of friends which does not include members of the opposite sex, gang members or terrorists.

"What time will you be home?" Note: the honest answer is usually the wrong answer from the young driver. This typically results in a negative response from the parent.

In the end the decision whether to let the teen use the car will be arbitrary and unrelated to any rationale.

As parents, Lorna and I handled this decision by telling our kids they could borrow the car as long as it was not needed by either of us. There was a small notebook in the car in which they entered the beginning and ending odometer reading and were charged ten cents per kilometre. This covered all the expenses, including gas. If they put gas in the car, they would enclose the receipt and the amount was deducted from what they owed. No questions were asked about where they were going. In the pre-GPS era there was little point in asking that question since it was virtually impossible to verify the answer. The implicit policy included not driving if they had been drinking, not going out of the country and not using the family sedan for mudding at the local drainage ditch. In retrospect, the last condition should have been stated more formally and explicitly… but I digress.

BOARDS, BUDGETS AND MIGRAINES

Some Boards are like parents arguing with their teen about the use of the car. Directors, like parents, ask irrelevant questions that give them a sense of being responsible and in control. Leaders, like teens, are hassled with questions that have little to do with anything. Eventually a decision is made that is tied to a mood, a pet peeve or a personal preference.

No single area of Board governance receives as much attention as the budget. Budgets are developed and questioned and redrafted and amended and resubmitted and tweaked and finally passed.

"But isn't that what Boards are supposed to do?" you ask. "What about our fiduciary responsibility as Directors?" (Whatever that is!)

First we need to clarify the term *fiduciary*. Fiduciary, used in the context of a Board's responsibility, has to do with the legal responsibility to manage certain assets and decisions on behalf of others. Being a Director on a Board is all about governance; and governance by definition is done on behalf of someone else. Part of the governance responsibility of the Board is to ensure that all the assets, including charitable donations, are properly handled.

FRETTING THE DETAILS

Let's look first of all at the whole concept of the budget itself.

A budget is a plan for how the Charity's money will be spent within a designated time

> Financial statements do not provide hard evidence of value.

frame—typically a twelve-month period. Budgeted amounts are often based on the projected actual numbers for the current year. Adjustments are then made to reflect changes in programming costs, salaries, and such, along with inflationary costs.

Financial statements do not provide hard evidence of value. They do not demonstrate that the money spent within the current year has been well spent or that the Charity availed itself of all the potential income sources that could have been reasonably accessed. It is what I call an "is" report. It is just a statement of fact.

What happens when the financial statements of the current year are used as a basis for next year's budget?

Suppose the cost for the previous year's cell phone use by the management team was $4,000. Based on a two percent inflation rate, that amount would be increased to $4,080. But how does the Board know that the $4,000 amount was reasonable in the first place? Is management subscribing to a cell phone plan which provides far more minutes than are being or should be used? Are a significant number of the minutes used for personal calls? Should the Board be performing an analysis of each cell phone bill?

> If the Board has not been able to verify that last year's money was well spent, then approval of next year's budget is not well founded.

What about utility costs? Does the office manager fail to turn down the heat or turn off the air conditioning when the office is closed, therefore inflating the utility costs? Is this something that the Board should look into? If so, what would that look like? Should the Board monitor when the heat is turned down or the air conditioning is turned off? Unless it invests unreasonable amounts of time and energy, how can it ascertain that the amount spent in the current year is being well spent?

If the Board has not been able to verify that last year's money was well spent, then approval of next year's budget is not well founded.

The result is a package of material on the boardroom table which is more overwhelming than enlightening. For the more mathematically or analytically inclined Directors, the budget is an opportunity to demonstrate their accounting acumen. For the majority of Directors this will be a tedious process. Budgets are presented with varying degrees of detail. For example, in a smaller Charity, the salaries may be broken down by individual employees while larger Charities often have just one number in the salary line.

Suppose the salary budget of a Charity is $410,000. As the Board begins to probe into that salary line, it is reminded that due diligence has been exercised. The HR Committee has reviewed each individual salary package, having justified any increases and how they compare to industry norms. Even if the Board accepts the credibility of the salary scale, the question of the competence of each employee has either not been confirmed or has been confirmed by the Leader, who by virtue of presenting the budget is implying that each employee is competent. Otherwise, why would the Leader agree to pay an employee they believe to be incompetent? Even if the Board assumes that the salary for each employee is reasonable and every employee is competent to do the job for which they have been hired, how does it know that each employee is needed?

How's your headache?

This leads to another question. Why is the Board approving the salary amount when the HR Committee has done the research? Is it just a formality? The Board cannot approve anything unless it has the clear option to withhold approval. To grant or withhold approval must be based on a criterion. Often that criterion is little more than a gut feeling that an amount "sounds okay." This is classic rubberstamping. In the end the Board might approve a $410,000 salary line

> The Board cannot approve anything unless it has the clear option to withhold approval. To grant or withhold approval must be based on a criterion.

without any criterion for making that decision other than someone else's recommendation—a recommendation that was not provided in the context of any terms of reference from the Board.

The Board now has a budget to review for which it cannot verify the reasonableness of some expenses:

- Is the cell phone bill appropriate?
- Is too much electricity being used?
- Is there good value for certain expenses?
- Are the employees competent?
- Are all the current employees necessary?

Let's look at another example of how a Board often approves a budget without the facts. Office supplies are often lumped into one line item. Suppose $2,500 has been approved for office expenses. It would be interesting to hear the response of the Board when it realizes that it has just approved the potential purchase of $2,500 worth of paperclips. There is no reason, other than common sense, why the Leader could not go out and purchase $2,500 worth of paperclips. That leaves no money in the budget for the purchase of paper to which the paperclips can be attached. The Board will be quick to point out the common sense factor, noting that it would be foolish to purchase so many paperclips without any paper.

The other extreme to approving $2,500 in office expenses without any reasonable policy, is to dive into the details of each item. This could include a list of how many paperclips will be purchased within the $2,500 budget and how much those paperclips would cost. Of course if the Board really believes it is exercising its fiduciary responsibility by going into this much detail, it should make sure paperclips are only purchased after three comparative prices.

Given these two scenarios, what is the alternative to rubberstamping and micromanaging the purchase of paperclips?

If the Board assumes the Leader will exercise common sense in the purchase of office supplies, why does it not say so? The Board could simply develop a policy to cover off this contingency. If the Leader's limitations to which we referred earlier include a Means limitation around office supplies, such limitation would be sufficient. A Means limitation policy might look like this: "The Leader shall not fail to ensure that the staff is properly resourced with office supplies necessary to carry out the administrative functions of the Charity." However, the Board may not be totally comfortable with *any reasonable interpretation* of this policy. Arguably the Leader could still purchase $2,500 worth of paperclips and $2,500 worth of staples because both paperclips and staples are necessary in the proper functioning of an office—in which case the Board could develop a more specific policy stating that:

> 1.0 The Leader shall ensure that the inventory of office supplies shall not exceed that which can be reasonably used within one year from the date of purchase.

> The middle ground of rubberstamping and micromanaging is tweaking.

I would submit that by the time the Board gets down to setting these types of policies, it should have some serious concerns about its Leader. Nonetheless you can see how a Board can approve an arbitrary number which is somewhat meaningless, rather than proactively approving a policy which controls reasonable expenditures.

The same can be said for income. It is presumptuous to base next year's income projections on last year's actual income with a small adjustment for inflation. It assumes that all revenue streams have been adequately tapped or that the Leader has given good overall leadership to fundraising initiatives.

One alternative to either rubberstamping or micromanaging is a move toward the middle. What does middle ground look like? Does a Board drill down on some items but not others? Does the Board have a look at each budget item without going into too much detail? If so, how is "too much detail" defined and who defines that? The middle ground of rubberstamping and micromanaging is tweaking.

Reflect back on what your Board has typically done. It may have drilled down to the granular details on such things as salaries or Sunday school supplies or insurance costs, depending on the particular passion of a particular Director. Why do some line items in a budget receive microscopic investigation while others are approved without so much as a passing comment? It grows out of the Board's misunderstanding of what is involved in looking at a budget.

The role of the Board is not to approve a specific dollar amount, but to approve the policies that generate the dollar

> The role of the Board is not to approve a specific dollar amount, but to approve the policies that generate the dollar amount.

amount. The Board can develop policies around balanced budgets and some cost controls and then let the Leader manage the finances. After all, the Leader was hired to lead and manage; so let them do it. Policy Governance is a model that allows for proactive policies rather than reactive decisions.

SUMMARY

In this chapter we have seen how the traditional way in which Boards approve budgets can raise some interesting questions. The Policy Governance model provides for carefully crafted and clearly worded limitation policies, thus allowing for appropriate controls on what the Leader cannot do while providing flexibility for the Lead-

> Policy Governance is a model that allows for proactive policies rather than reactive decisions.

er. The end result is less tedium for both the Board and the Leader. If the policies are properly monitored, the Board and the Members can have confidence that the financial integrity of the Charity is intact.

Many Charities run into a Leadership crisis which can create long-term relational fractures between the Board and the Leader, which can ultimately lead to misunderstanding, confusion and hurt among the Members. In our next chapter we will look at how the likelihood of that can be significantly reduced.

?

Question #11

How Does a Board Relate to Its Leader?

Making Sure No One Is Surprised

"I supposed this should go to the Board for approval."

"I think I know what the Board wants but I'm never quite sure."

"At my annual review I am often blind-sided by things the Board is unhappy about or things it wanted done that I wasn't aware of."

"Sometimes I get instructions from the Board, sometimes from a committee and other times they come from a Director."

"When it comes to hearing from the Board, I can't tell the difference between a suggestion and a command."

"I had lunch with one of the Directors who was upset about some things. He says that others on the Board feel the same way, but I've only heard it from him."

These lines are all too familiar when dealing with the relationship of the Board to the Leader.

WHO'S THE BOSS?

In the last few chapters the case for proactive, established policies for the Leader has been made. However, policies regarding the way a Board relates to the Leader are also required. One of the characteristics of Policy Governance is the way in which the performance of the Leader is always evaluated by their adherence to the proactively stated Ends policies and their progress toward achieving the stated Ends within the carefully crafted and clearly worded Executive Limitation policies. Performance evaluations within this framework allow the Leader to clearly understand what is expected without any surprises. Because both Ends and Executive Limitations are expressed by policies which have been passed by the Board, everyone is reading from the same page.

HOW THE LEADER GETS THE MESSAGE

> The Board will deal only with the Leader as it connects with the operations of the Charity, and will do so only through written policies.

The way in which the Board relates to the Leader is spelled out in its own set of policies which can be referred to as Board-Management policies. These policies explicitly state that the Board will deal only with the Leader as it connects with the operations of the Charity, and will do so only through written policies.

It is the Board and not individual Directors that interacts with the Leader. The Leader has seen in the Board-Management policies that directives will come only from the Board as a whole. Instructions will not come from an individual Director, who may have an individual agenda, or from the Chair, unless speaking on behalf of the Board. An instruction may be communicated to the Leader by the Chair, but that communication will be a Board directive and not the instruction of one particular Director.

On the occasion when an individual Director interacts with the Leader, care must be given not to send the Leader a confusing message by implying that the comments are reflective of a Board position.

I serve as the Chair of a Board where I am periodically contacted by the Leader and asked for my opinion or perspective on a decision he needs to make. In calling me he will often preface his question with, "I am calling you as a friend." This introduction is a gentle reminder that he is not asking for permission, nor does he see my opinion as being binding on him. This scenario is easier to deal with because it is the Leader who is initiating the conversation. When the Chair or another Director approaches the Leader, the possibility for misunderstanding is heightened.

The Board's only connection with the operations of the Charity is through the Leader. The Board as a whole or an individual Director must not do an end run on the Leader by going directly to an employee. This does not mean that a Director cannot have a casual and caring interaction or lunch with an employee, but caution needs to be exercised so that

> The Board's only connection with the operations of the Charity is through the Leader.

the employee does not see the Director as exercising an "employer" or "boss" role.

There are times when the Board may want to monitor employee satisfaction or an employee may become aware of an issue of which they believe the Board should be made aware. There is a process for these situations to be addressed. Remember, this book is a 40,000-foot view of the governance terrain and to delve into these exceptions would require than we reduce our altitude. So we will leave this for a different flight.

One of the Board's policies as it relates to the Leader is that any instructions regarding Ends to be accomplished or Means to be avoided will only be issued through written policies. Verbal statements don't count. Suggestions don't count. Hints don't count. The only instructions that count are policies that have been passed as motions at a Board meeting.

The Board has only one employee and the Leader has only one boss. Individuals and organizations can get derailed by lack of clarity regarding roles and responsibilities. Having this understanding reduces the likelihood of any confusion.

In some Board-Leader relationships, the Leader can be seen as reporting to the Chair. In the next chapter I will elaborate on the connection of the Chair to the Board. Briefly stated: In the Policy Governance model, the Board as a whole is the employer—not the Chair.

How is the Leader Doing?

So far the Leader understands the Ends that need to be accomplished and the Means that must be avoided. It is unfair now for the Board to introduce

> The Board has only one employee and the Leader has only one boss.

additional expectations that it has not already stated. The Board has agreed to accept *any reasonable interpretation* of the Executive Limitations it has given to the Leader. As such, the performance of the Leader is the same as the performance of the organization. Through the monitoring of Ends and Executive Limitation policies, the Leader shows that the intended benefits are being produced and the targeted beneficiaries are being reached and the prohibited Means are being avoided. An annual evaluation can permit minor concerns to be noted and compensation to be adjusted, but the Leader should never have their performance evaluated against criteria that have not already been stated in a written policy.

Monitoring Reports

Part of the Board's commitment to operate with openness and clarity is seen in how it reviews Monitoring Reports. In an earlier chapter we looked at Monitoring Reports in the context of Executive Limitations. We saw that a report consists of four parts:

1. Policy
2. Interpretation

3. Data

4. Declaration of compliance

If there is non-compliance, the Leader will state why there is non-compliance and what will be done to move back into compliance.

I have talked about the *any reasonable interpretation* principle. The Board agrees in its Board-Management policies to accept any interpretation that would be given to a policy by a reasonable person. Remember it is the Leader and not the Board who interprets a policy. Therefore the Board cannot arbitrarily decide it doesn't like a particular interpretation just because that interpretation does not suit its purpose. If the Leader offers an interpretation that is reasonable, but is beyond what is acceptable to the Board, the Board needs to amend the limitation on a go-forward basis. It cannot change a policy retroactively.

The Board must let the Leader know when the Monitoring Reports are due. The Board may want a monthly Monitoring Report as it relates to financial statements, whereas a report on the system used to back up files may only be requested once a year. In any case the Leader should have the schedule, including a deadline stating when the Monitoring Report needs to be sent to the Board.

Summary

This chapter has focused on the rules by which the Board relates to the Leader. Everything is outlined in a policy that the Board agrees to live by as it relates to its Leader. The Board should not be blindsided by *unmet* expectations nor should the Leader be blindsided by *unknown* expectations.

I have talked about how the Board has clear policies regarding its expectations for the Leader and limitations on the Means that can be used by the

> The Board should not be blindsided by *unmet* expectations nor should the Leader be blindsided by *unknown* expectations.

Leader to advance the Ends of the Charity. Unfortunately, Boards often do a poor job of evaluating themselves. In fact, many Boards have no policies or guidelines that govern their own behaviour. In the next chapter we will look at the policies that the Board imposes on itself.

Question #12

How Does a Board Grade Its Own Performance?

Setting the Rules for Board Conduct and Sticking to Them

BOARDS ARE OFTEN *LESS THAN THE SUM OF* their parts. A Board can be made up of Directors who are exceptionally brilliant, highly educated, extremely competent and successful business owners. None of them have achieved success by being inept. How is it then that six to twelve of these individuals can come together, make decisions and conduct business in a way that bears no resemblance to their behaviour in professional life or the business world? A lobotomy is the only procedure that would explain how so much capacity can dissipate so quickly.

A Board can be much more effective and efficient when it develops good *Board Process Policies*. These policies define how the Board agrees to function and are reviewed regularly to ensure that the Board holds itself accountable to them.

Remind Me... Why Am I Here?

If you were to ask a Director if the Board they are on is doing a good job, I would submit that

> Boards are often *less* than the sum of their parts.

many would be hard pressed to answer the question. It is impossible for someone to know if they are doing a good job, if they don't know what their job is.

The role of a Board is very basic. It just needs to make sure that what should happen, happens, and what shouldn't happen, doesn't happen. In making sure these things happen assumes that a Board knows what should happen (stated Ends) and not happen (prohibited Means).

There is a lot of stuff in that one suitcase, so let's start unpacking.

> The role of a Board is very basic. It just needs to make sure that what should happen, happens, and what shouldn't happen, doesn't happen.

We will assume that by this time the Board has heard from its Members and is able to articulate its Ends. It knows what should happen. It is clear what benefits are to be achieved by the Charity, who the beneficiaries are and that the cost for those benefits is reasonable. "Because *The Caring Kitchen* exists, indigent people in the community will have regular access to nutritious meals which can be provided at a cost that is less than an equivalent restaurant meal." We know:

- who will be benefited—indigent people in a specific community

- what the benefit is—regular access to nutritious meals
- the cost—less than a restaurant meal

There is no point in providing meals at a cost greater than a restaurant meal. Otherwise it would be more cost-effective to raise the money and pay the restaurant directly. Earlier we spoke about another potential End—that citizens of the local community have an opportunity to make a difference in the lives of those less fortunate. For the purpose of this example, we will set that aside.

We have here a Board that understands its purpose and is governing on behalf of its Members, as well as its Moral Owners, to make sure that what should happen, happens, and what shouldn't happen, doesn't happen.

A Board should not act as if it has the unfettered right to do what it wants because it is the Board. The Board as a whole, as well as its individual Directors, does not exist to advance its own agenda. It is not there to serve and support the Leader. A Board *must* support its Leader, but that

> A Board *must* support its Leader, but that is not its purpose. A Board does not exist to assist with administration or tell the Leader how to manage the organization.

is not its purpose. A Board does not exist to assist with administration or tell the Leader how to manage the organization. The Board is there to serve as a connection between the Members and the Leader to ensure the Charity stays on track. Staying on track includes making sure the Ends of the Charity are achieved while making certain unacceptable Means are avoided.

Diversity is a Good Thing

> If every Director agrees with every idea brought forward, there is only a need for one Director.

Boards are made up of individual Directors who bring a variety of perspectives. If every Director agrees with every idea brought forward, there is only a need for one Director. This does not mean there should be arguments and disputes just for the sake of having more than one opinion, but robust debate on issues is a positive thing. Opinions should be voiced clearly and thoughtfully, but held lightly. Keep in mind that at some point an idea is going to be voted on and if you find yourself in the minority, don't make personal what isn't personal.

We Don't Need an Accumulation of Experts

Sometimes when Directors are being recruited for a Board, consideration is given to areas of expertise. Having a former teacher on a school Board or a missionary on a mission Board provides opportunity for others to hear the perspective of someone who has had direct experience with the Ends of a similar Charity. At other times when Directors are being recruited, special consideration is given to having a lawyer or an accountant who can bring their area of expertise to the Board. Again this can be a real asset to the Board as expertise may increase the understanding of the Board. However, it is the Board that makes decisions and its decisions should not be based on the opinion of an expert while the rest of the Board passively acquiesces to the specialist.

WHAT IS THE CHAIR'S JOB?

The role of the Chair, sometimes referred to as the Chief
Governance Officer, needs to
be understood by the Chair and
the Board. First let's look at the
most important part of this role.

The Chair makes sure the
Board stays on track with its
own policies. Referring to the

> It is the Board that
> makes decisions and its
> decisions should not be
> based on the opinion of
> an expert while the rest
> of the Board passively
> acquiesces to the
> specialist.

previous section, it is the responsibility of the Chair to ensure the Board does not use the expertise of an individual to
prevent the Board from having to use its collective judgment.

Another role of the Chair is to make sure there is diverse
and robust debate by not allowing one or two Directors to
dominate the meeting or not allowing other Directors to remain quiet and uninvolved.

The Chair is responsible to put together the proposed
agenda for the Board meeting. This can be done in cooper-
ation with the Leader but it is ultimately the Board's and not
the Leader's agenda. Note that it is a *proposed* agenda which
needs to be approved by the Board at the beginning of the
meeting. Under Policy Governance it is the Chair's responsibility to make sure the only issues on the agenda are those
that fall within the responsibilities of the Board. Means issues
should not be on the agenda other than the consideration
and approval of Monitoring Reports. The only other time for
Means discussions is around the consideration or clarification of current Executive Limitations.

A Board will typically operate using Robert's Rules of Order. Before you reach for the Tylenol, let me comment on Robert's Rules of Order. These rules are the widely accepted authority that ensures meetings function in an orderly fashion and decisions are arrived at properly. There are very few people who are fully proficient in the use of Robert's Rules of Order, but don't sweat that. It is only important that a Board agrees that there is a final authority in determining how something is handled in the event of a dispute. The official Robert's Rules of Order website is www.robertsrules.com.

The Chair is usually the one who speaks to outside parties about various Board positions. When the other Directors understand that, and they are asked by an outside party such as the media to comment on the Board's position, they know to defer to the Chair.

But the Chair is Not All-Powerful

The Chair is not the boss of the Board and doesn't get to make their own rules or run the Board on their own terms. The Chair is one of the Directors who is accountable to the Board under the terms of the policies to which we have just referred.

One of the challenges a Board faces is the tendency to defer to the Chair. This can sometimes lead to the Chair having an inordinate number of meetings with the Leader and thereby creating a perception that the Chair and the Leader run the Board meetings. The Chair certainly has a uniquely empowered role as it relates to their responsibilities, but the role itself does not place them above the Board.

A Board Secretary Does More Than Take Notes

There was a time when someone (often a woman) possessing good writing skills and a penchant for detail became the default Board Secretary. Hopefully we have moved beyond the stereotypes of the mid twentieth century.

The primary role of the Board Secretary is to ensure the accuracy of Board records, including the minutes taken at a meeting. Nothing requires that the Board Secretary take the minutes. A Board may want to engage the services of someone who is not on the Board to take the minutes, allowing all the Directors, including the Board Secretary, to enter into the deliberations of the Board. Note that the Board should not use an employee such as an administrative assistant or executive assistant to take notes. The role of this individual as an employee should not be compromised by having them present at a Board meeting. Regardless of who takes the minutes, the Board Secretary is responsible for the accuracy of the minutes, including the assurance that they have been accepted by the Board, signed and kept in a safe place.

Whoever is taking the minutes needs to be somewhat—shall I say—obstinate. Sometimes a Director will say "Yeah, I'll move that" without providing a clearly worded motion. The Director making the motion should always say, "I move that…" and then dictate the motion. By doing so, it gives the Board Secretary time to write down the exact wording. While it is the role of the Chair to insist that the motion be clearly worded, sometimes that does not happen. In that case, the Board Secretary needs to be adamant in seeing this is done before the motion is deliberated and voted on.

I mentioned that the Board needs to be aware of the important role of the Secretary in maintaining the integrity of the Charity's records. Often Board minutes of a previous meeting are sent out just before an upcoming meeting. By then few Directors can recall what was specifically decided and those who remember may be guilty of rewriting history. A best practice is to have the minutes approved at the end of the meeting in which they are taken. The person taking the minutes should not have to leave the meeting and try to recall conversations and construct wording. If it is practical, have the minutes taken on a laptop and projected on the wall at the end of the meeting. Any amendments or omissions can be made then and there. The minutes can be accepted. Done and done.

Another role of the Board Secretary is to ensure that official Board documents such as the founding documents and by-laws are both current and available. This does not mean the Board Secretary has to have them in their possession; they simply need to know where the documents are kept, such as the office of the Charity. Remember, it is the ultimate responsibility of the Board, and not management, to ensure the integrity and security of the corporate documents.

The role of the Board Secretary is a very important function such that the work of the Board Secretary should be reviewed at least once a year.

Review and Reflect

If a Board has its own policies about how it should function, those policies need to be reviewed at least annually to ensure the Board is in compliance with its own policies. This evaluation will ascertain whether the Board is addressing Ends issues or getting bogged down in the discussion of Means. The annual evaluation should include the role of the Board Chair, the Board Secretary and individual Directors.

- Are there policies and procedures the Board agreed upon which are not being fulfilled?

- Is the Board tenacious in its review of Monitoring Reports?

- Are there conflicts of interest and if so, have those been declared?

- Is it treating the Leader fairly and in a way that is consistent with its own Board-Management policies?

It is appropriate to ask the Leader if they believe the Board is functioning in a way that is consistent with its own policies.

A Board must be uncompromising, inflexible, obdurate, unyielding and obsessive in reviewing its own Governance Process policies, Ends policies, Executive Limitation policies and Monitoring Reports of the Leader.

> A Board must be uncompromising, inflexible, obdurate, unyielding and obsessive in reviewing its own Governance Process policies, Ends policies, Executive Limitation policies and Monitoring Reports of the Leader.

Summary

In this chapter we have looked at the role and responsibility of the Board, its Chair and its Secretary. We saw that a Board needs to understand its role in governing on behalf of its Members. Once the Board understands its role, it develops policies to ensure it operates in a way that is consistent with that role. Then it regularly checks up on itself.

It is essential that organizational vocabulary means the same thing to everyone within a Charity. In the next chapter we will look at some terms, give them a definition and see how they fit within the culture of a Charity.

Question #13

Vision, Values, Mission...
What Do They Mean?

Simple Definitions for Relevant Terms

LUGGAGE IS SOMETHING YOU USE TO KEEP everything together when taking a trip. The actual suitcase itself is not necessary unless you have something to put in it. Imagine, however, packing for a trip and not having a suitcase. Toiletries are tucked under one arm, pants and shirts are stuffed under the other and your underwear is jammed into your pockets. This may be okay if you are traveling by car, but less functional if you are flying. While luggage itself does not have any intrinsic value, it sure is nice to be able to carry all you need by just grabbing a handle.

Mission statements, vision statements and a statement of core values are like pieces of luggage. They have no value in themselves, but they are handy for carrying the *raison d'être* of the Charity.

It seems that every Charity thinks it needs some luggage. It may not have anything substantial to put in the suitcase, but at least it has a suitcase. For example, if a Charity does not have a mission statement, then a committee needs to be struck to develop one. And while the committee members are hard at it, they could consider a vision statement as well; or is a mission statement and a vision statement the same thing? In the end a few cute or cumbersome phrases are cobbled together,

> Mission statements, vision statements and a statement of core values are like pieces of luggage. They have no value in themselves, but they are handy for carrying the *raison d'être* of the Charity.

placed in a document and buried in a file cabinet, never to be seen again. That is as useful as buying a suitcase to take on a trip and stuffing it full of whatever can be found because that's the thing to do when going on a trip. Like taking too much luggage or not enough luggage, nothing is more overvalued or undervalued as a mission statement.

A mission statement does not detail every reason for which the Charity exists, but like a suitcase, a mission statement needs to be unpacked.

Why a Handle?

Throughout this chapter I will be making reference to these terms as "handles." Handles are typically attached to larger and bulkier items to assist in carrying them. A handle that is not attached to anything is utterly useless. Nor is a handle of any use if it is attached to something that doesn't need to be carried. If you have bulky items such as some luggage but no handle, you will quickly discover the importance of a handle. Once you have grabbed the

> Nothing is more overvalued or undervalued as a mission statement.

handle, you can carry your entire luggage without having to wrap your arms around it. Remember the precursor to roller bags? There were small wheels on the bottom of the suitcase with a plastic strap that was hooked onto the front of the suitcase so you could drag it through an airport. If you walked too fast the suitcase would weave back and forth like an unsteady drunk, eventually falling over or veering into the path of some unsuspecting traveller, taking them out at the knees. I recall leading a short-term mission trip on which someone brought along one such suitcase. After we had arrived at the airport in Mexico City I was asked if this type of suitcase was okay. My sensitive response was, "As long as you're carrying it, any suitcase is okay."

> Sometimes the handles of the Charity are similar to the pioneer efforts of the roller bag suitcase;—a good idea in theory but functionally less than useless.

If you are the owner of a restaurant such as the one operated by Eric to whom I referred to earlier in the book, a mission statement is not necessary. A Charity functions on a much different basis. It must be able to clearly and succinctly communicate its values and its mission. Sometimes the handles of the Charity are similar to the pioneer efforts of the roller bag suitcase;—a good idea in theory but functionally less than useless. A mission statement may sound good in a boardroom but not translate well into real life. If your Board is going to spend time developing handles, make sure the handles perform the function for which they were intended.

Right Handle, Wrong Suitcase

As basic as this may sound, it is important that the right handle be attached to the right suitcase. It is possible to have a handle that is comfortable and allows you to carry the suitcase with ease. However, if the comfortable handle is carrying the wrong suitcase, you will end up at some point along the journey with luggage you never intended to have and with clothes that don't fit.

I worked with a Leader who decided the Charity he was leading needed to define its mission-vision. I eventually asked him what the phrase "mission-vision" meant to him. He responded by saying that he really didn't know the difference between a mission and a vision so he included both terms just to be safe.

Let's start with some common terms and assign definitions to them. If you read a variety of books on the subject of mission statements and vision statements you will get a variety of opinions. Let me suggest that your Charity should have a glossary of corporate vocabulary so that when a term is used, everyone will understand what it means. I am less concerned about the actual words and more concerned that when using those words, they mean the same thing to everyone associated with the Charity. You can call it *purple horse* or *pink lettuce* for all I care—just make sure that when those

> Your Charity should have a glossary of corporate vocabulary so that when a term is used, everyone will understand what it means.

terms are used everyone knows what they mean. Also make sure these terms are located in places where they are easily accessible to both the Board and the employees.

Let me suggest some definitions you may find helpful for your Charity. It won't be as creative as *purple horse* or *pink lettuce*, but it will give you a start. This glossary will be developed by starting with the most foundational terms and building on them, one by one.

STATEMENT OF FAITH

The core of many religious charities is the Statement of Faith. It is important to know how the fundamental tenets of the faith impact what the Charity is seeking to do. Everything about a church, a Bible camp or a Christian school grows out of assumptions around matters of faith.

The Statement of Faith answers the question *What… What do we believe?* Statements of Faith vary from Charity to Charity. Some are quite generic and will successfully encompass a variety of theological and doctrinal perspectives. Other Statements of Faith such as those developed by a church tend to be much more specific. Regardless of the specificity, the Statement of Faith is the foundational conviction of a Charity. Everything done from the outset is based on the Charity's beliefs about God and people.

MISSION STATEMENT

Earlier we talked about Ends as the results for which the Charity exists, the beneficiaries of those results and the cost/value. Ends clearly define results outside of

> The Statement of Faith answers the question *What... What do we believe?*

the Charity and are *not* what a Charity does. On the other hand a mission statement *can* include what the Charity does. It is critical not to confuse a mission statement with Ends.

A mission statement answers the question *Why... Why do we exist?* It may begin with "We exist to..." And go on to describe the basic service or ministry provided by the Charity.

One of the first things I did when launching *Ted Hull Consulting* was to develop a mission statement, even though my consulting service is essentially a one-person operation. I do not have staff that I need to keep focused on the mission nor do I have a Board that requires a mission statement. Why then would I bother with a mission statement? Why do I need

> A mission statement answers the question *Why... Why do we exist?*

a handle? Because I need to be able to grab the handle that carries the reason for which my consulting service exists. I must quickly be able to know why I am doing what I am doing. I

must know when I get out of bed in the morning why I will do certain things, take on certain projects and say no to other opportunities. My mission statement is primarily for my benefit. Hopefully as others read it, it will help them to understand why my organization exists, but I primarily need it for me.

The Mission Statement of *Ted Hull Consulting* is *to facilitate the organizational and relational advancement of churches and charities so they can move from where they are to where they want to be.*

That's the handle. It helps me to carry my mission. Mission statements do not need to be, nor should they be, comprehensive. A good mission statement, like a suitcase, will require some unpacking. So let's open up the *Ted Hull Consulting* suitcase.

First, my mission is *to facilitate*. I do not exist to do for a client what a client can do for themselves. I do not typically come in and tell a church or a Charity precisely what it needs to do. I seek to make whatever challenge or process a Charity is facing easier to address.

My mission is to facilitate *organizational and relational advancement*. The purpose of this book in part is to facilitate organizational advancement. I want to see churches and charities advance their ministries because they are well organized and well governed. While being well organized and well governed does not guarantee a Charity's success, it will increase the likelihood of success. Part of my mission as well, is to facilitate relational advancement by helping organizations deal with conflict or misunderstanding between employees, or between a Leader and a Board.

One of the things I look for when assessing opportunities for service is whether the church or Charity sees itself as needing to move in a particular direction. I am not invigorated by meeting with a Charity just to present a generic seminar. I am not wired to simply come in and offer my services with little sense that what I say is going to move the church or Charity in a specific direction. My experience in my in-

When we are up to our waist in alligators, it is difficult to remember that the original intention was to drain the swamp. Mission statements help us stay focused when we are in the swamp.

dividual and marriage counselling practice over the years has been similar. It is disappointing (read: frustrating) when a client comes in for counselling with no idea of what they hope to see accomplished. This can happen if someone has been mandated to go for counselling or a spouse has been threatened with the termination of a marriage if they don't get counselling. Of course there are always some directions to move in a situation like that, but that must remain for another book. There were times when counselling clients would come in and have a sense that something was wrong in their relationship but they were unable to identify it. I would sometimes begin by asking: If I could wave a magic wand and change something, what that would be? Of course I had no such wand and change was seldom easy, but it challenged them to define, according to my mission today, what *advancement* would look like. Charities are in some ways the same. There can be a vague, nebulous sense that something is wrong but the Board may not be able to articulate it. All it knows is that *advancement* is necessary.

Including the terms *churches and charities* in my mission statement reminds me that my primary focus is not-for-profit organizations.

The word *they* is used intentionally and strategically. I do not see my role as the one who moves a Charity from where it is to where it wants to be. I assume that if I properly facilitate the process and if there is a clear understanding of what *advancement* means, then the Charity will move from where it is to where it wants to be.

I have just used a few pages to unpack a twenty-five word mission statement. Clearly a mission statement does not need to be comprehensive but it

> A mission statement must be *compelling or people won't be interested in it.*

must be a handle with which I can carry my organizational luggage. A wise sage once said that when we are up to our waist in alligators, it is difficult to remember that the original intention was to drain the swamp. Mission statements help us stay focused when we are in the swamp.

What should a mission statement look like?

First, a mission statement must be *compelling or people won't be interested in it.* You don't want a mission statement that leaves people responding with a "yeah so what…" attitude. You particularly do not want that ho-hum attitude among people who are employed by or volunteering with

> A mission statement must be *concise or people won't remember it.*

your Charity. People must be clear about the mission of the Charity. It must be front and centre. Make sure that employees and volunteers have learned it, understand it and can repeat it by memory. On the flip side, this means that the mission statement must be compelling.

Second, a mission statement must be *concise or people won't remember it.* Someone has suggested that a mission statement should fit on a T-shirt. Some mission statements including mine would need to be printed in very small font or on a very large T-shirt. The point is—it's a good rule of thumb.

You want people to be able to rattle off the mission statement virtually without thinking about it. It needs to become part of the corporate vocabulary. At the same time, in your quest to have it concise make sure that it is not reduced to a tagline. The tagline for *Ted Hull Consulting* is *so you can better serve*. It reduces my mission statement down to five words. While it is concise, it would not qualify as a mission statement according to our definition. If my tagline was my mission statement, people would have very little understanding of why *Ted Hull Consulting* exists. Who can better serve? How can they better serve? Who will they better serve? What is being served? Hopefully it looks good on my letterhead and my business card, but it will hardly help people understand why *Ted Hull Consulting* exists. Let me clarify: I'm not saying that taglines aren't valuable. I love great taglines. One of the best I've seen is the one used by FedEx in its sponsorship of a race car in NASCAR: *FedEx...where every day is race day*. In fact I received a bumper sticker at a race and stuck it on my toolbox. Just make sure that concise is not confused with cute; because cute can be confusing.

> A mission statement must be *credible or people won't believe it.*

Third, a mission statement must be *credible or people won't believe it*. It is pointless to develop a mission statement so outlandish that it is an insult to people's intelligence or so grandiose that it is an embarrassment for people associated with that Charity. Avoid using superlatives such as *largest, biggest* or *most*. One of the challenges created by this type of language is realistic measurement. Even if it could be measured, the likelihood that it will be the biggest, the largest or do the most is negligible. A mission statement is not a marketing ploy. It just answers the question as to *why the Charity exists*.

Fourth, a mission statement must be *complete or people won't understand it*. Mission statements are not easy to create. In endeavouring to develop a mission statement that is concise, you can err on the side of incompleteness. A mission statement should completely summarize everything your Charity hopes to do. Suppose *The Caring Kitchen* operates an inner-city mission providing food, clothing, housing, addiction treatment programs and a residential program. If its mission statement only makes reference to feeding people, it is incomplete. There is always the tension between being too long to remember and too short to be meaningful. With that in mind, make sure your mission statement is complete; otherwise people will not understand the mission of the Charity. Communicating to yourself and others why your Charity exists is the reason you go to all the work of developing a mission statement in the first place. A final word: Complete is different than comprehensive. A good mission statement will briefly state why the Charity exists without going into great detail.

> A mission statement
> must be *complete*
> *or people won't*
> *understand it.*

CORE VALUES

Keep in mind as we move forward that we are starting with the most basic terms and moving outward. When the mission has been defined by answering the question "Why do

> Core values answer
> the question *Who…*
> *Who are we?*

we exist?" we want begin identifying those values that define
the Charity. Core values answer
the question *Who… Who are we?*
The term "core value" is often
misunderstood. If core values define *who* the Charity is, then
those values must distinguish *that* Charity from *other* charities.
I am not suggesting the core values of a particular Charity are
unique to that Charity. To be unique would mean that the values of that Charity are not values owned by any other Charity.
At the same time they must be values that are not common to
every other Charity. For example a Christian Charity might
list the Bible, prayer or trust in God as core values. According to our definition of a core value, the Bible, prayer or trust
in God are not core values. This should grab the attention of
fundamentalist Christians everywhere. However, before you
consign this book to the dustbin of heresy, hear me out.

Remember we talked about a Statement of Faith? Your
Statement of Faith may include references to the Bible as
being the authoritative Word of God. If the authority of the
Bible is taken seriously then it will include the high value of
prayer as indicated in the Bible. The Bible also underscores
both instructionally and anecdotally the importance of trusting God. Any good Christian Charity should highly value
the Bible, prayer and other values consistent with the Christian faith. Those values should go without saying in terms
of being core values; so make sure they go without saying.
Those values belong in a Statement of Faith.

When listing the core values of the Charity, they should
be specific to the Charity. One of the core values of *The Caring*

Kitchen may be stated as, "We value the equality of all people." You might say that the equality of all people should be a value of any Charity and that is true. But for *The Caring Kitchen*, that value is particularly significant because it will not allow anyone to make disparaging remarks about other visitors, including remarks about race, body shape or colour. The impact and effectiveness of *The Caring Kitchen* is dependent in large part on the assurance that anyone who comes there will be treated with the utmost respect. A large suburban church in an affluent part of the city may identify excellence as one of its core values. That particular church believes that its capacity to impact those who come, particularly non-church suburbanites, will depend in part on its level of excellence. Does that mean *The Caring Kitchen* does not value making a quality sandwich for its patrons? No. But the existence of the inner-city soup

> A core value must be believable.

kitchen may not be dependent on excellence, whereas the value of excellence is vital when a large, upscale suburban church is trying to impact its community.

A core value must be believable. The worst thing in stating a core value is to have the Charity function in a way that undermines the credibility of that core value. A mission organization may say that it values the indigenous church. It could expand on that value by saying that the effectiveness of an indigenous church in a developing country is dependent on the raising up of national leaders. If you got close to that mission organization and found that national leaders were constantly being undermined, disempowered and second-guessed, you could rightfully conclude that what

> A Charity cannot have a core value that can be externally undermined or assailed.

the organization says is a core value is in fact not a core value at all.

A Charity must be able to control its core values. Restated, a Charity cannot have a core value that can be externally undermined or assailed. Remember that a core value defines the Charity. If someone external to the organization can change that core value then in essence the Charity can be redefined. When developing a list of core values, it is important to examine each one through the lens of whether someone on the outside could stop your Charity from embracing that core value. Once a Charity has embraced a set of core values it must be prepared to adhere to those values in the face of any challenge, obstacle or enemy. If the core values are eroded, the Charity essentially ceases to exist as it is. Core values define the character and DNA of the Charity.

> If the core values are eroded, the Charity essentially ceases to exist as it is.

Core values must be understood by those who are directly responsible for ensuring the core values as stated are the ones that are embraced. Every key person in the Charity must not only know what the core values are and agree to accept those values—they must be passionate about those values. A cursory saluting of the flag is not acceptable. Core values must not be put in a box and set on a shelf. They must have a dynamism that drives the activities of the Charity.

A core value will be followed up with a *therefore*. We talked about a potential core value of *The Caring Kitchen* as being the equality of all people. When stating the equality of all people as a core value, one must assume a practical demonstration of that value. Such a core value may be stated as, "We value the equality of all people and therefore every person who comes to *The Caring Kitchen* will be treated with respect and free from the fear of discrimination or insult by any employee, volunteer or patron." Staff and volunteers joining the Charity will be told about this core value, will understand the

> Core values must be understood by those who are directly responsible for ensuring the core values as stated are the ones that are embraced.

practical implications of this core value and will be passionate about it. They will ensure that anyone coming in for a meal is given utmost respect. This will be front and centre in the dining room and constantly reiterated at staff meetings. Everyone will know that the equality of all people is a core value of *The Caring Kitchen*.

VISION STATEMENT

Remember that problem of distinguishing between a mission statement and a vision statement? Here is the key difference. While a mission statement tells us why a Charity exists, a vision statement answers the question *Where… Where are we going?* Aubrey Malphurs, an authority on leadership, defines a vision as a clear, compelling picture of the future as it can and must be. [3] (Malphurs 100)

A vision statement paints a clear picture of what a Charity will look like either at a determined or undefined point

> A vision statement
> answers the question
> *Where... Where are we
> going?*

down the road. A good vision statement will be clear to the people who hear it and read it. It will not be couched in vague terminology such as *more* or *better*. *The Caring Kitchen* may have a vision statement that paints a picture of what the Charity will look like in a specified timeframe: "In five years, *The Caring Kitchen* will be a safe, accessible and spacious facility, with the capacity to feed 500 meals each day to homeless people in the inner-city." Can you picture a building that is safe from rowdiness and abuse, is easily accessible to people who do not have their own transportation and where they can move around with a cup of coffee without slopping it onto other people? This should provide significant motivation to the Members of the Charity, the Board, the staff and volunteers as well as those who are invited to donate to the Charity.

A vision statement must be compelling. It should have a "wow" factor to it. People who hear the vision statement can see the vision and are compelled to become involved at whatever level they are able. They may ask how they can get involved in the construction of the facility, supply materials or serve as a volunteer.

The vision statement is a picture—not in the sense of a photo, but rather like an architectural sketch. An architectural sketch of a senior's home may include landscaping, lighting and drawings of cars in the parking lot. The completed building will not look exactly like the sketch due to changes in the details. The shape of the windows may be different, the doors could be on the left-hand side of the building rather than the right-hand side and the landscaping will be different. Nevertheless the drawing provides a picture of what can be anticipated when the construction is complete. The same is true about a good vision statement. Some of the details will be different but the general idea will be the same.

A vision statement is always about the future. It often begins with "We will be…" A good vision statement must not describe what the Charity is currently doing or accomplishing. It describes something that will be different in the future.

Beware of developing a vision statement that is either easy to accomplish or totally unrealistic. I recently spoke with the development director of Habitat for Humanity in a large city. I did not specifically ask what their vision statement was for the next five years. However, she told me that in five years they were planning to build twenty-five homes per year. She went on to tell me that twenty-five homes was a very

> A vision statement must be compelling.

significant increase over what they were currently doing. It was not just one or two homes more per year. A vision statement that invites involvement should not be something so grandiose that people quickly lose heart and abandon the vision altogether. On the other hand, if it is only an incremental adjustment to what is currently being accomplished, the vision will not be inspiring.

Describing a good vision statement as something that must happen, is not to suggest that it must happen exactly as it is described—rather the future must be different than the present. If a Charity can settle for where it is now or what it is accomplishing, it does not need a vision. An inspirational vision statement will include something that must be different than it is now.

> If a Charity can settle for where it is now or what it is accomplishing, it does not need a vision. An inspirational vision statement will include something that must be different than it is now.

Some time ago I was speaking to a group of leaders about the need to have a good vision for the future. Someone asked me about the vision I had for *Ted Hull Consulting*. He was wondering if I saw my consulting services expanding to include associates and an administrative pool on the 30th floor of an office tower. I admitted my vision was much less expansive and expensive. It was one that saw me narrowing the focus of my services while deepening my impact. This book in fact is one realization of my vision for *Ted Hull Consulting*. Keep in mind that vision statements are far more important for charities, which must attract broad-based involvement, than it is for a one-person consulting firm.

Vision statements can be regularly changed as a particular part of the vision is realized. To describe something in a vision statement that has already been accomplished is meaningless. Keep the vision statement clear and current. Leave out initiatives you are no longer willing or able to pursue.

Vision statements can be longer than mission statements. They may include an entire document or the transcription of a presentation. In any case, it must communicate something worth pursuing because of the difference it will make.

STRATEGIES

If a good vision statement tells us where we are going, then strategies answer the question *How… How do we get there?* Remember that as we use these terms we are moving out concentrically. The items closest to the centre of the circle are the ones which are least flexible. As we work our way toward the perimeter of the circle, the

> Keep the vision statement clear and current. Leave out initiatives you are no longer willing or able to pursue.

things we talk about are more likely to change over time. For example it is prudent to never change a Statement of Faith except to reword it for clarity or contemporary terminology. The Charity was created to execute a mission and that mission defines why the Charity exists. That should not change. Core values may be tweaked or amended over time but they need to be solidly in place. A vision statement is going to change over time. As milestones or benchmarks are reached and the desired picture of the future is realized, the vision statement must change to accommodate a new or renewed vision. The strategies employed will be constantly changing.

I have referred to Means in the context of Policy Governance. Ends describe the benefits resulting *from* the Charity and the benefactors *of* the Charity. Means are everything else that a Charity does. While strategies

> Strategies answer the question *How… How do we get there?*

are similar, they are not to be confused with Means. Strategies, such as projects, programs and initiatives, are the specific methods used to realize a vision. Means include operational processes such as developing budgets and providing purchasing guidelines. Strategies focus on the program activities of the Charity which will constantly be changing to ensure the Charity's mission is pursued and its vision brought to fruition.

Make Sure to Check Your Luggage

Airports serve to remind us that many suitcases look familiar. Any time spent huddled around a baggage carousel as scores of black suitcases snake their way past you will reinforce that reminder. Regardless of how similar suitcases appear on the outside, the contents of each are vastly different.

Creating handles to carry the valuables of a Charity can sometimes be like New Year's resolutions. They seem like a good idea at the time, but all too soon atrophy in the mundane activities of January. Let's look at a few reasons for failing to act on the good intentions contained in various statements.

My, What Unique Handles!

At this point you will have some clarity regarding terminology and guidelines for attaching certain handles to the luggage that carries important items. However, there are at least two reasons why these handles are not used. First: the handles are more cosmetic than convenient, more ornamental than practical. While the mission statement may be appealing and the vision statement compelling, they do not reflect why the Charity exists or where it is going.

Right Suitcase, Wrong Handle

I recently consulted with a church which wanted to re-evaluate their mission and how they intend to impact their community. When asked what their current mission was, they quoted their mission statement: "*To see un-churched people become fully devoted followers of Jesus Christ.*" When I asked them what they were doing to bring in un-churched people, they acknowledged that most of the people coming were disillusioned and disenfranchised church attendees from more traditional churches in the area. I pointed out that while there was nothing wrong with their mission statement or their mission, there was little correlation between the two. They needed to re-examine their mission. I encouraged them to do a thorough re-evaluation of their ministry to determine if their mission statement had been adopted only because it was catchy and popular. Maybe the church had deviated from its original intention of reaching out specifically to un-churched people and gravitated to those who had previously connected with another church. Using our suitcase analogy, it was like having a functional suitcase, but instead of using it to carry travelling clothes, it was being used to carry the kitchen sink—something for which it was not intended.

No One Will Carry the Luggage

The second reason for handles being ignored is because there is no real ownership of the mission statement as it reflects the mission of the Charity. This is more prevalent among Directors who want the flexibility of having the Charity engage in whatever project appears to be expedient or exciting at the time. In helping Charities with mission statements, I sometimes hear someone suggest, "What if we want to do something that is not part of our mission statement?" There are three options:

1. Change the mission statement.

2. Change the mission.

3. Refrain from doing things that are not part of the mission (usually the wisest option).

Mission statements are or should be a reflection of the mission of the Charity and serve to keep the focus of the Charity inside the suitcase.

I was approached by the head of a department of a Charity to assist them in editing some manuals that clearly were in dire need of editing. Knowing I had written some articles and was in the process of writing this book, he believed I would be able to assist them in this project. I must confess I was very tempted to accept the challenge. But when reflecting on my corporate mission statement, I realized I would deviate from priorities that were consistent with my mission of facilitating the organizational and relational advancement of churches and charities. As such I reluctantly said no to the invitation. My commitment to adhering to a carefully thought through mission statement prevented me from doing something I would like to do, but was inconsistent with my mission. I need to regularly challenge myself to function within the confines of my mission and remain focused despite appealing opportunities which ultimately distract from my brand. This is extremely important when there are Members and Moral Owners to which a Board is accountable.

FAILURE TO HAVE THE MISSION IN VIEW

Charities can spend a lot of time coming up with various symbolic handles, only to put them on the shelf or bury them in a filing cabinet or on a hard drive. Having gone to the effort of developing these handles, they need to be in plain view. This may include printing the mission statement, vision statement and core values on various organizational documents or neatly framing them for display on a wall. Even these measures will not guarantee the handles will be used to carry the corporate luggage of the Charity. I strongly recommend that the Board pull out each of these handles on a regular basis for review.

> My commitment to adhering to a carefully thought through mission statement prevented me from doing something I would like to do, but was inconsistent with my mission.

Once I was flying back to Canada from Central America and was delayed by numerous cancelled flights. My itinerary had me departing Guatemala City at 7:00 AM but that flight was cancelled. Eventually I got a flight that rerouted me through various cities, eventually landing me at 1:40 AM the next day in Chicago. Knowing that I needed to leave in but a few hours and being the frugal traveller, I chose to overnight in the main departure terminal area. I was exhausted and all by myself except for a few maintenance workers. To make sure no one stole my suitcase or backpack, I ran my luggage padlock through the handles of my luggage and attached it to the bench on which I "slept." As it was, my "sleep" was disturbed every five to ten minutes with monotonous recordings reminding me that I was in a no-smoking terminal and not to leave my baggage unattended. I did not lock the handles to protect *them* from being stolen. I was only concerned about the contents of my luggage.

In the same way, a Board should not be concerned with protecting mission statements and vision statements for the sake of the statements themselves. To ensure that the missional and visionary integrity of the Charity is maintained, have the handles tested and reviewed on a regular basis.

FAILURE OF ACCOUNTABILITY

I have taken the risk of articulating my mission statement in this book. In so doing, I have invited informal accountability to the extent that any reader can ask if I am continuing to function in a way that is consistent with my mission statement. Because I am a sole proprietor, any accountability for consistency is voluntary. A Charity on the other hand, needs to allow itself to be held accountable for adherence to its core values, mission statement and vision statement. A Charity cannot be held accountable for something that it has not formally documented. These statements need to be available for inspection by any of the Charity's stakeholders. As we move to the handles of vision and strategies, visibility may be less important to the owners but equally as important to the Board and the Leader.

I keep a list of everything I could conceivably need when I go on a trip. I know how many dress shirts, T-shirts, casual pants and jeans I will need. Depending on the purpose and length of the trip, my challenge is less about what to take and more about deciding which suitcase to use. Hopefully as a Charity has laid out what it believes and what it wants to see accomplished, this chapter will help in choosing which suitcase it needs and will help in attaching the right handles.

Summary

We have reviewed some of the terms used by charities which are intended to encapsulate its interests regarding *what* it believes, *why* it exists, *who* it is, *where* it is going and *how* it is going to get there. We have used the analogy of handles (terms) attached to suitcases (statements) which need to be unpacked and used.

In our next chapter we will have a specific look at churches and how their structures require some special considerations not faced by other charities.

?

Question #14

How Are Churches Different From Other Charities?

The Importance of Gatekeepers in a Church

So far I have referred to charities as a general term to describe organizations that include mission agencies, not-for-profits, para-church ministries and churches. In this chapter I want to look specifically at local, autonomous churches. By autonomous I am not excluding churches that are part of a denomination but rather churches that, whether or not they belong to a denomination, have flexibility in the way they protect their doctrines and provide spiritual leadership and oversight to their congregation. This is not intended to be a theological discourse on church leadership or the recommendation of a particular model of church governance. Rather, this chapter recognizes that churches are a unique type of Charity.

A church in Canada does not need to be registered. There is nothing to prevent a group of people from meeting together in their homes as did Christians in Bible times and continue to do in many parts of the world, including Canada. If such a church chooses to become a registered Charity, other laws come into effect. Some espouse that the Bible is the sole authority for church governance and that books such as this are unnecessary or irrelevant at best.

> Churches cannot become registered Charities and then claim the Bible as their sole authority on how they are structured.

Some may go so far as to suggest what I am saying is heretical. Churches cannot become registered Charities and then claim the Bible as their sole authority on how they are structured. They can't have it both ways. This chapter is intended to briefly look at how these potentially conflicting positions can be brought into balance. But before we sort that out, let's look at some of the ways in which churches are different than other Charities.

CHURCHES ARE THEOLOGICALLY DIFFERENT

Churches are different than other charities because by their very essence they are identified by their theological and doctrinal beliefs. I referred in the previous chapter to Statements of Faith, which are included in the basic documents of some charities. A mission agency can change its Statement of Faith without essentially changing what it does or to whom it ministers. On the other hand if a Pentecostal Church alters its views on the Holy Spirit or a Catholic Church abandons the authority of the papacy or a Plymouth Brethren Church gives up the weekly celebration of the Lord's Supper, it undermines its doctrinal uniqueness.

Churches Are Functionally Different

People who become involved in a Charity usually do so for altruistic reasons. Their involvement may include giving of their time, expertise or finances. Their volunteerism is seldom given in exchange for what they can get out of it. That does not mean they do not receive a personal sense of satisfaction or even delight in their involvement, but it is not typically the original motivation. Conversely, churches are viewed by many

> Churches are different than other Charities because by their very essence they are identified by their theological and doctrinal beliefs.

of their constituents as a place where they receive care. Isn't it interesting that the very people who serve other charities expect to be served by the church.

Churches today are facing issues that were not contemplated even two or three decades ago. Today's parents need to make sure their preteens enjoy the children's programming to avoid a campaign to change churches. Churches did not face this dilemma when Sunday school was not an option for the children. Whether the kids were happy had little or no bearing on Mom and Dad's decision about which church the family attended. Now the children's programming must be interesting *and* biblical, entertaining *and* edifying. If a church is not up to the standards of a family, that family will quietly or not so quietly move on to another church. Ergonomically padded seats, theatre-quality projection and concert hall lighting are a requirement for any church that seeks to attract new Members. Please understand, I have sat on enough hard pews in enough churches without air conditioning or a decent sound system not to appreciate some of the enhancements we enjoy now. In reality, the expectation placed on the church to produce consumer satisfaction can move it toward doctrinal compromise.

Churches Are Relationally Different

People are generally more attached to their church than to a non-church Charity. An individual can be involved in a variety of non-church Charities with equal passion. On the other hand it would be difficult for a person to relate to a variety of churches in the same way. Churches are more than just a place to serve. People refer to their *home church*—a place where they believe they will be correctly taught about God and the Bible. As such they become protective of the beliefs and practices of their church, seeing any changes as a threat to their sense of spiritual security. Some people would even see certain changes as a risk to their personal identity which is closely connected to their denominational heritage. Congregants often speak of their *church family*—people to whom they look for support in times of difficulty.

A governance structure must be in place that allows the Members of a Charity to direct the organization through Directors appointed to a Board, who then usually employ the services of a Leader. This is still important in a church which needs to make all types of decisions, from changing a program to changing locations. When it comes to protecting the doctrinal fundamentals of a church, there is a need for what the New Testament refers to as Elders. For the sake of our discussion, I am referring to them as the gatekeepers who serve as the guardians of the tenets of the faith. It is interesting to note that churches in the New Testament do not appear to have been democratic. Spiritual leadership was not left to a popularity contest or to those who were the most verbal or the most well-known.

How can the rights of the Members of a church which has chosen for financial reasons to be a registered Charity be balanced with the need to protect the fundamental truths of that same church?

I realize that I am touching on a topic about which some readers will have strong convictions and passionate opinions. Setting human subjectivity aside, some will maintain their viewpoint is supported by biblical authority. I am writing from personal conviction, personal experience and a personal viewpoint and without complete biblical objectivity.

I spent the first thirty years of my life in a conservative Plymouth Brethren Assembly. The guidelines for church leadership were presented as being something that could and should be clearly understood if taken from a biblical perspective. Those years have inescapably shaped and influenced my perspective on church leadership. Since then I have heard the advocates of many different church practices, each conversation possessing varying degrees of passion and conviction. I will limit my comments to the points I believe are germane and vital.

> When a new Member joins a church and formally agrees to its Statement of Faith, they should do so because of personal convictions that align with the beliefs of the church.

Any church that is able to issue tax receipts is a registered Charity subject to the same laws as non-church Charities.

As I meet with church Leaders, I regularly remind them that the ultimate legal authority for what goes on in a church lies with its Members. Members can ultimately pass resolutions that can potentially undermine the basic truths of the church. Statements of Faith and the purposes of the church, as found in its documents, can be amended if enough Members wish to see that happen.

Churches are generally different from non-church organizations in that the tenets of their faith are foundational to their identity as a church. It is their Statement of Faith that makes them unique. To change their Statement of Faith can make such a fundamental change that the church ceases to be the church it was.

A registered Charity provides an opportunity for Members to vote for or affirm Directors or Elders. How is that opportunity balanced with the need to have gatekeepers in the church who have a responsibility to protect the doctrinal elements that have been acknowledged and agreed upon by the Members?

Let's begin with the Members. At one point, the Members agreed to certain positions which provided for a doctrinal foundation. When a new Member joins a church and formally agrees to its Statement of Faith, they should do so because of personal convictions that align with the beliefs of the church.

It is possible for *The Caring Kitchen* to change its constitution and purposes so that a soup kitchen now becomes a skateboard park for suburban youth. All it would require is a sufficient percentage of the membership to vote in favour of such a change along with government approval. The minority who are not in favour of the change will be disappointed and maybe even angry. They may even redirect their support and resources to a similar Charity as *The Caring Kitchen* or create a new Charity.

In the case of a church, there must be individuals in positions of recognized authority who are gatekeepers of the doctrinal positions of that church. While these spiritual values may not be held with equal passion by everyone, they should not be eroded by apathy or indifference.

> In the case of a church, there must be individuals in positions of recognized authority who are gatekeepers of the doctrinal positions of that church.

I would suggest that the Board of Directors or whatever term is used to describe the body of gatekeepers in a church must not only govern on behalf of the Members, but do so in a way that ensures the doctrines of the church are protected.

The challenge is finding the balance between having the Bible as the primary voice of the church gatekeepers (rather than the capricious voices of Members who may never have owned the doctrinal values of the church), and complying with the legal requirements of being a registered Charity and allowing Members to vote. These need to be carefully considered in the governance structure of a church.

WHAT ABOUT THE SMALLER CHURCH?

While there are more large churches now, a majority of people still prefer a church where they can easily connect with everyone and where the Leader knows each congregant by name. Scraping enough money together to pay a pastor, having church members serve for years on the Board and making sure enough people volunteer are some of the bigger challenges faced by a smaller church. Accordingly, there may be a tendency to shrug off much of this chapter and this book as being relevant only to the larger church.

Though many of the dynamics are different, the principles I have addressed in this book are as valid and applicable to a smaller church as they are to multi-million dollar charities. In a smaller church the need remains for clearly stated expectations regarding the overall direction of the church and what Means should not be used to pursue that direction.

Any church that pays its Leader will have expectations of that Leader and an evaluative process. In many cases the expectations have not been formally agreed upon, much less written down. As a result, the Leader is evaluated informally based on standards which are developed arbitrarily. Discontent with the Leader may begin in the back row of the sanctuary rather than the boardroom of the church. "He wasn't nice to my aunt." "She never asks me to sing." "The sermons are too long." When the Board is no longer able to hold back the tide of discontent, the Leader is relieved of their duties.

Another scenario is the Leader who comes in assuming they know what is best for the church and the community. Advice is dismissed and cultural context is ignored. Consequently, the evaluation of the Leader is whispered behind closed doors. Any formal or public evaluation may be avoided, but the failure to meet unspoken expectations is noted at kitchen tables.

Both a Board and its Leader are entitled to clear expectations of Ends to be reached and Means to be avoided. Clarity around these issues will go a long way to minimizing the misunderstandings and subsequent hurt.

Bear in mind that in a smaller church many people are often required to wear more than one hat. The parent of a Sunday school student may be the same person who sits on the Board. The greatest challenge is wearing the right hat in the right situation. When they are upset about their child's Sunday school teacher showing up late, they are only a parent and as such should not be using their board position as leverage. Nor should a Board meeting be the time to complain about their child's Sunday school teacher.

Smaller churches would do well to bring in someone from the outside that has no history, undue bias or vested interest to assist in bringing some of these concerns to the Board so they can be addressed openly and constructively.

The matter of governance in the smaller church deserves far more attention that it has received in this book. It affects more people and more charities than many of the organizations with a more formalized governance structure; but that discussion can be had in another book.

Summary

In this chapter we have underlined the importance of having gatekeepers who serve the church by protecting its doctrinal distinctives. At the same time we have seen that a church which decides to register as a Charity needs to be aware of the need to comply with the legal requirements associated with registration.

Now that you have had a helicopter ride and seen the governance landscape, you may be deciding if you want to land and become involved in the governance of a Charity. Our next chapter will hopefully provide you with some clarification.

Question #15

How Do I Know If I'm Board Material?

Questions to Ask Before Signing On

THE FACT THAT YOU HAVE MADE IT THIS FAR through the book suggests you have some interest in governance; and that is a good starting point.

I have served on a variety of Boards over many years with my motivation for doing so varying as much as the Boards themselves. My first experience was fuelled by a specific expertise I thought I could bring. Because the Board needed Directors, it was more than willing to accept my offer to serve. Soon after joining the Board, I realized it was not interested in my expertise and my capacity to influence fellow Directors was minimal. Some of the Directors had been on the Board for many years and subtly assured me that my not-so-subtle nudges toward change were not warmly welcomed. Once I knew I was on the wrong road, I took the first exit ramp I could find.

Not long after this experience, I was invited to sit on a Board comprised mostly of older men who were themselves asked to be Directors based on their long association with the Charity. Being the youngest person on the Board, I made it my personal mission to keep the meetings interesting by opposing any motion for which I could find even an obscure reason. One particular meeting provided me with opportunities to live out my dream. The Board meeting had broken for dinner subsequent to three motions which I had not supported. It was apparent to me that this group was not used to having anyone vote against any motion. I recall while sitting at dinner, one of the more sensitive Directors asked me if I was okay. I smugly assured him that I was doing fine while asking him why he was concerned. He pointed out that I had been voted down on three different motions and that I must be feeling quite hurt. While my immature arrogance may have clouded my desire to see the cause of the organization advanced, I did have enough sense to realize that the passing of motions was based on a majority vote. I went on to assure him that while I had voted against all three motions, I was willing to accept the judgment of the majority.

> Your decision to become a Director does not mean you have to vote in favour of every motion; but nor should you be motivated by serving in an obstructionist role.

Your decision to become a Director does not mean you have to vote in favour of every motion; but nor should you be motivated by serving in an obstructionist role.

Currently I serve as a Director on two Boards, both of which operate under the Policy Governance model. While I do not come with unique expertise, I also do not believe my contribution is unnecessary or redundant. Hopefully I bring a special perspective to each Board. I am privileged to serve as the Chair of one Board with a group of women and men who each bring their own strengths. Some of the Directors are more analytical while others are more constructively critical. Some have a penchant for detail while others are big picture people. No one individual dominates the discussion and the Board would be diminished if even one of the Directors was not at the table.

I have been spoiled by serving on Boards that operate under the Policy Governance model. In fact, I would not consider serving on a Board that operates on the traditional model of guessing at decisions it is supposed to make, micromanaging details of specific interest or rubberstamping issues it does not understand. I could not function where items were presented for approval but for which I had no criteria for granting or withholding approval.

> I could not function where items were presented for approval but for which I had no criteria for granting or withholding approval.

Assuming you have an interest in governance overall, you will want to consider the governance model with which you are most comfortable. Having determined that, you can ask informed questions of the individual or Board that is asking you to serve as a Director.

It is vital that you begin by looking at your motivation for wanting to serve as a Director. If you can learn from my history of serving on Boards, you may save both yourself and others some disappointment and frustration.

Your decision must never be fuelled by the motive of being in a position where you can implement the changes you have always wanted to see. This is a not a rare incentive especially for those who want to serve on a church Board. Their motivation can be as innocuous as wanting different music in a Sunday morning service or as toxic as crusading to have a pastor removed.

> Your decision must never be fuelled by the motive of being in a position where you can implement the changes you have always wanted to see.

Another thing you want to consider is the motivation of the individual or Board that is asking you to serve as a Director. Many Boards including church Boards are hard up for Directors, in which case, they may be looking for a warm body to fill a spot at the table. This begs the question as to why you would want to be on the Board when so many others are not interested. It could be a rubberstamp Board where meaningful discussions and debates are not encouraged. It could be a Board where endless debates take place over trivial items while the macro issues are never addressed.

You may be recruited to serve as a Director because of your influence or personal profile. In this case the individual asking you to serve may be more passionate about having you on the Board than you are in serving on the Board. This may feel flattering at first, but you will soon become bored if the Charity is not engaged in a ministry that captures your heart.

In the introduction I referred to the preponderance of men serving as Directors. A Board exists to serve on behalf of its Members, who in many cases are comprised equally of women and men. As such, while women may be actively recruited because of their gender they should also be recruited for their capacity to hear from and reflect the values of female Members as well as the governance expertise they can contribute. There is a thin line, but a line nonetheless, between recruitment that is motivated by the appropriate need for gender representation and the unspoken paternalistic pressure for a "token" woman on the Board. Do not hesitate to ask that tough question.

Don't fail to solicit answers to any questions you want to ask. After all, you are taking on a significant responsibility, including a considerable investment of time. Ask yourself if this investment of time and resources is a greater priority than other possible opportunities.

So what should you expect (read: insist on) before you agree to sit on a Board? Following is a checklist of questions to which you should be able to answer yes to yourself before you answer yes to someone else.

1. Do you agree with its Statement of Faith? This applies particularly to a church Board. Not only must you understand and assent to it, you must be prepared to defend it.

2. Do you understand its mission? Make sure the person asking you to sit on the Board can clearly articulate the mission. If they don't understand the mission, you certainly can't be expected to understand it. And if

you can't understand it, how can you support it?

3. Are you passionate about what the Charity is seeking to accomplish? If you have the time and qualifications to sit on a Board, do not sit on one that has a mission about which you are not passionate.

4. Can you buy into the vision of the organization? Not only must you understand why the Charity exists, you must know where it is going and be in agreement with it.

5. Do you understand your responsibilities as a Director? You have been entrusted with the responsibility of representing the Members, and as such it is vital to understand that you are not just a passive spectator. Read any of the books on governance that I have referenced in the introduction.

6. Have you asked questions regarding any unspoken expectations of the Charity or other Directors? For example are you expected to give a certain amount, fundraise or participate in all the fundraising events associated with the Charity? These and other expectations are sometimes implied but not verbalized. Then later some Directors or Members of the Charity are offended when the new Director does not live up to the expectations others have.

7. Do you know the governance model under which the Board operates? Don't begin to play the game until you are clear about the rules. Asking if it is a Policy Governance Board is a good place to start; however, do not assume that because someone tells you they use Policy Governance that they necessarily understand what that means. They may simply mean that the Board governs by policies, without any understanding of Policy Governance. Finding these things out in advance can save a lot of pain and avoid areas of disagreement down the road.

8. Will you be provided with a governance binder? Ask for a copy of all the policies, founding documents and minutes from the past year, along with any other important documents.

9. Does the Charity carry Directors and Officers insurance? If the answer is no, this will be a clear indication regarding the level of sophistication of the Board. You do not want to be part of a Board that does not carry Directors and Officers insurance. Directors can be held personally liable for failing to exercise due diligence in overseeing the activities of the Charity. These can include mismanagement, wrongful

dismissal of an employee, unpaid wages, financial losses and failure to comply with any applicable statutes.

10. Do you have the gifts and the temperament necessary to be a Director? Two vital qualities of a Director are the capacity for passionate deliberation and collaborative decision making. You must be able to clearly articulate your opinions and perspectives. This must be separated from any personal agenda you may have. Some people are very sensitive and as such do not want to debate vigorously either because they don't want to risk upsetting someone else or being challenged about their own perspective. Also you want to be careful not to use any powers of personal persuasion to intimidate or cause the voices of other Directors to be quieted. People will not always see things your way, regardless of how clear your perspective is to yourself and how clearly you have communicated it to others. At times you will need to soften your view to allow for consensus. There will be times when you will believe strongly enough about an issue to vote

> Two vital qualities of a Director are the capacity for passionate deliberation and collaborative decision making.

against it. How you vote must never become personal.

11. Do you have the time and the family support to be a Director? Most of us do not have gaps in our schedule waiting to be filled by Board meetings. So you need to consider what you are willing to give up to serve in this role. A Charity worth serving deserves the best you can bring to the meetings. Make sure you have the time and the energy, as well as the support of your family.

If you can answer yes to these questions, you can consider taking on this responsibility with the information you need, the enthusiasm you will inject, and the wisdom you have to offer.

SUMMARY

Hopefully this chapter and this book have enabled you to carefully consider your role in the governance of a Charity. You

> How you vote must never become personal.

should by now have an understanding of how charities function, including the role of the founding Members, the Board and the Leader. You know there are significant fiduciary responsibilities and legal requirements that need to be considered. Remember, the Charity is not an asset with which you are free to do with as you wish. It is entrusted to you by the Members to ensure that the intended recipients are appropriately benefited. You have been introduced to Policy Governance as a model for governing charities. You have seen the importance of understanding corporate vocabulary that ensures common and consistent understanding of the terms in use. You are aware that those who govern as Leaders in a church have a unique function.

All this combined should let you know if you have what it takes to be a significant contributor to the successful governance of a Charity.

In our final chapter we will identify those times when it can be helpful to have an outsider facilitate the advancement of charities so they can move from where they are to where they want to be.

?

Now That I've Read the Book, Why Do I Need a Consultant?

The Benefits of the Right Consultant at the Right Time

THERE ARE TWO GOLDEN RULES TO BEING a successful consultant. The first is you never tell anyone all that you know.

When I was sixteen years old I spent the summer selling Fuller Brush. For the more youthful readers, Fuller Brush was a company that sold household cleaning supplies door-to-door. While my venture was not a financial success, it was invaluable for providing me with some career direction. While I did not know what I wanted to be when I grew up, I was clear about what I didn't want to be.

When speaking with potential clients, I don't try to sell governance restructuring. Not only am I inept at sales; no one wants to buy a governance restructuring process. I prefer to begin by asking, "What is wrong with the current structure?"

There is no point in trying to point a Board in a new direction unless it sees a need to improve its current structure.

Incremental Change is Not the Answer

A number of years ago in Canada there was a political party formed called the Rhinoceros Party, which was intended to inject some humour into the electoral process. One of the planks in its platform was to have Canadians start driving on the left-hand side of the road. But rather than implement the change all at once, it would be phased in over five years starting with motorcycles in the first year, cars in the second year, light trucks in the third year, buses in the fourth year and finally the fifth year with tractor-trailer units.

One of the challenges in governance restructuring is doing it in a piecemeal way. Using a traditional model of Board governance concurrent with a Policy Governance model may not produce the carnage of the incremental change from driving on the right side of the road to the left side, but it could be almost as frustrating.

Do not underestimate the idea that moving toward Policy Governance is a different game than the one typically played by Boards. It is a move from management being one step removed from the Board to the Board being one step removed from its Members and ultimately its owners. It removes the gray zone between the Board and the Leader and creates a clear line so that both the Board and the Leader are aware of their responsibilities.

Moving in this direction requires someone who can outline the process from beginning to end before the process is started. My recommendation is to begin with a consultant presenting an overview of Policy Governance to the entire Board. This could take about a day and a half. For example the Board could meet with the consultant on a Friday evening and Saturday morning, leaving the afternoon free for questions and answers regarding the impact on the Charity of moving to Policy Governance.

Following that, any Director could call the consultant and ask any lingering questions that require further clarification. This process should not go on for more than a few weeks, at which point it is time to call a special meeting of the Board. At that meeting the Board needs to make a decision whether to move forward or not.

One of three things is likely to take place:

1. The Board completely buys into the model with a "When can we start?" attitude.

2. The Board is not prepared to move toward Policy Governance, at which point it either continues with its current process or moves in a different direction.

3. A contingent of the Board is either strongly opposed, or does not see the need or the advantage of making such a quantum shift. In some cases these Directors may resign saying that they are not going to stand in the way of what others believe is in the best interests of the Charity, even if objecting Directors do not see the advantages of moving toward Policy Governance.

> Initiatives to change the governance process of a Charity are often born more out of frustration with the current model than a vision for the future of the Charity.

Broad-based support is vital for moving ahead with Policy Governance. Once the decision has been made to move down this road, the Board cannot afford to keep revisiting the question or second-guessing itself as to whether Policy Governance is the model it wants to embrace.

Having made the decision to move forward, someone will need to give overall direction to the process. As the Chair or as a Director, you may have decided you want to lead a change in the governance process of your Board but I would suggest that someone who is not part of the Board is better positioned to lead the Board through the process. Initiatives to change the governance process of a Charity are often born more out of frustration with the current model than a vision for the future of the Charity. The last thing a Board needs at this stage is more frustration. If the Board begins to back away from the restructuring process, you will be very frustrated and possibly the other Directors will become frustrated with you. Consequently it is critical to bring in someone from the outside that can facilitate the process from beginning to end.

Take Your Time — Do it Well

As mentioned earlier, it is important that the actual transition to Policy Governance take place at a given point in time rather than spreading it out. Set aside some dedicated blocks of time to work on this rather than squeezing it into a number of Board meetings in between other agenda items.

START WITH EXECUTIVE LIMITATIONS

Having made the decision to move in the direction of Policy Governance and having engaged someone to assist in the process, the Board's first action item is to develop the Executive Limitation policies. The consultant should only serve as a coach and allow the Board to begin to use its understanding of Policy Governance to discover what level of detail it wants in the various Executive Limitations. That level is reached when the Board is willing to accept *any reasonable interpretation* the Leader may apply to any particular limitation.

It may appear at first that because the Board is developing the Executive Limitation policies, which are Means that would be unacceptable for the Leader to use, it would be ideal if the Leader was not part of the process. This concern is valid if you believe the Leader would use their influence to "limit the limitations"; although having that concern may tell you something about the Leader. Assuming there is a good relationship between the Board and the Leader, the Leader can be there to assist in the process. For example there may be some Executive Limitations which should be included or implications to having others limitations the Board has not already considered. A Board should want input from the Leader, given the understanding that the Leader is one of the greatest assets the Board possesses.

An Executive Limitations policy is not a document that needs to be couched in legalese. It should be easily understood.

However, do not confuse *easily understood* with a *casual use of words*. Policies should be carefully crafted so the intention of the Board and the understanding of the Leader are not compromised. In spite of everyone's best efforts, misunderstandings may materialize after the first Monitoring Report in which the Leader interprets the policy differently than the Board originally intended. In the context

> Do not confuse *easily understood* with a *casual use of words*.

of a trusting relationship, this should not create any trauma. The Leader may have provided a reasonable interpretation of the policy which did not reflect the intentions of the Board. When that happens the Board simply needs to revise the Executive Limitation to provide clarity.

This will be an ongoing cyclical process: the Board develops an Executive Limitations policy, the Leader interprets it, which then requires the Board to clarify the Executive Limitation which in turn allows the Leader to give a more acceptable interpretation.

ANY REASONABLE INTERPRETATION

Once each Executive Limitation has been developed, the Board must ask itself if it is willing to accept *any reasonable interpretation* of the policy as it is written. It is unacceptable to impose a limitation or expectation on the Leader which the Board has not already stated in its Executive Limitation policies. Remember: the only limitations by which the Leader is bound are those formally passed by the Board. The Board cannot evaluate the compliance of the Leader based on Board expectations that have not been articulated as Means to be avoided.

A good consultant should assist the Board in clarifying its wording and asking the "any reasonable interpretation" question.

Your Board may want to know if there is a set of Executive Limitations *out there* that can be photocopied rather than going through the laborious process of developing its own policies. The definitive answer is yes and no. Templates for specific policies can be found in the books referenced in the introduction, notably the titles by Carver and Oliver. That is the "yes" part of the answer.

There are some things that characterize all Boards. Every Board exists to govern on behalf of its Members to make sure that the Charity accomplishes what it should and to make sure that what shouldn't happen doesn't happen. Nonetheless each Charity and each Board is unique both in terms of the Charity itself as well as the emphasis the Board wants to place on particular limitations. Medical doctors are capable of working on thousands of different individuals because there are characteristics common to all human beings. If all human beings are basically the same then why does a doctor need x-rays? If you are wondering the same thing, the next time you see a doctor, try walking in with a folder of x-rays taken of someone else. In the same way, Executive Limitations tend to cover off the same general areas such

> It is critical that each Board tailor its Executive Limitations to reflect its own values and concerns.

as the treatment of staff, financial planning, financial integrity, asset protection and emergency secession. Because the limitations that each Charity's Board will want to place on the Leader will be different, it is critical that each Board tailor its Executive Limitations to reflect its own values and concerns.

Board-Management Policies

Developing good Board-Management policies requires the Board to clearly state how it is going to relate to the Leader. The Board must agree that it will only address the Leader through formal policies and not in an ad hoc, arbitrary or reactionary way. It must also provide a schedule for receiving Monitoring Reports.

Board Process Policies

Board Process policies describe how the Board agrees to function and hold itself accountable to its declared modus operandi. The Board must bind itself to its commitment to review Monitoring Reports. In so doing, some things the Board should be looking for are:

- A reasonable interpretation of the policy by the Leader that the Board can accept.
- A comprehensive interpretation of the policy, i.e. one that does not interpret just a portion of the policy.

- A commitment to auditing the data. For example: the Leader may declare the Charity is sufficiently insured and provide a copy of the insurance policy. This does not mean the Board cannot look further. Additional monitoring may include contacting the insurance agent to ensure the information given by the Leader indicating sufficient coverage is consistent with the opinion of the agent.

The Board must be extremely diligent in reviewing Monitoring Reports.

ENDS POLICIES

The Ends policies are vital to the Charity. They spell out the reason for the very existence of the Charity. Ends policies are usually the most challenging to develop due in part to the fact that Boards are unaccustomed to thinking in terms of Ends.

Boards often complain they spend too much time talking about administrative details and not enough about the long-term goals of the Charity. Policy Governance has the advantage of not allowing the Board to spend time talking about Means issues. As much as the Board wants to develop proper Ends policies, the default drift is toward talking about Means. Considerable discipline

> Ends policies are usually the most challenging to develop due in part to the fact that Boards are unaccustomed to thinking in terms of Ends.

is required to avoid becoming involved in Means discussions once the Executive Limitations have been made.

Ends are not something about which Boards typically spend much time thinking. Boards will talk about developing a mission statement (why a Charity exists) or creating a vision (where a Charity is going). Talking about what the Charity is going to *do* or where it is going to go is typically a Means issue. Ends talk about results achieved and people benefited.

> A Charity does not exist for anything that it *does*.

Remember that a Charity does not exist for anything that it *does*. It exists for the benefit of those who are outside the organization and that benefit is identifiable and ultimately achievable at a reasonable cost. When a Board gets into the *Means* of food purchasing, volunteer management or leasing arrangements, it has started down a road that only the Leader should be on.

What About Consulting Fees?

Ah! Finally the question you've been hoping I would answer.

Based on the topic of this book, let's assume that the consultation has to do with governance restructuring or at least governance clarification.

Herewith a caution regarding consulting fees. Any consultant that starts off by telling you how much the service will cost is already appealing to your sense of economy. Remember that in consulting as in life, if you want economy you have to be prepared to pay for it. The fact that you have been able to engage the services of a consultant for a rock bottom price is not necessarily a point of honour for a Charity. Imagine a Chair announcing to the Board that the new consultant is the cheapest one they could find. When driving across a river it is small comfort to be reminded that the contract for the bridge was let out to the lowest bidder. Conversely a less expensive consultant is not necessarily ineffective in the same way that someone who is expensive is not necessarily the best.

Some consultants charge by the day or the hour. The advantage of a daily or hourly rate is the consultant knows they will be paid for the exact amount of time spent working for the

> Remember that in consulting as in life, if you want economy you have to be prepared to pay for it.

client. The advantage to the client is that the relationship with the consultant can be terminated at any point. Some consulting projects lend themselves well to that type of arrangement. For example the process of facilitating in a conflict situation can last anywhere from a few hours to a few months, in which case charging by the hour is the most advantageous for both the client and the consultant.

When assisting a Charity in a governance restructuring process, I am reluctant to charge by the hour or by the day. Agreeing on a flat rate for the entire process is much better for the client and the consultant. There are three basic reasons for this.

As a consultant I have a good idea of what is involved in the course of understanding where a Charity is, where it wants to go and the facilitation process. The heavy lifting takes place in the early stages of the process as the Board becomes acquainted with Policy Governance and as policies are developed. Just getting the Board up to speed and having Policy Governance in place is not the end of the task. I always assume it will take at least a year from the beginning of the process until the Board has made one complete revolution through its governance cycle. With that being the case, I want to be available to the Chair and to the Leader to assist them in walking through the challenges they will invariably face.

The second reason is that I do not like to be under pressure to ensure a project is completed within a certain number of hours or billing a client for every conversation. The temptation for a consultant working with a Charity on a limited budget is to cut corners by not dealing with situations which would otherwise be covered if there was not a per hour fee.

The third reason is a substantial benefit to the client. The Charity knows going into the process what will be delivered and what the cost will be. I typically charge for the introductory presentation which may be done on a Friday evening and Saturday. Following that, if the Charity decides to move ahead, a flat fee can be negotiated.

How Does a Charity Know if the Consultant is Competent?

After an initial conversation and the introductory presentation, the Charity may have a good idea if the consultant is capable of facilitating the process of governance restructuring. One of the best ways of exercising due diligence is to request references from charities for whom the consultant has done similar work.

"Is your Charity better off now than it was before you engaged the services of a consultant?"

"Did the consultant provide the services that were agreed upon?"

"Was the consultant interested in understanding the unique dynamics of your Charity?"

"Was the process completed in a timely manner or did you sense that once the contract was signed, the consultant was more preoccupied with lining up new clients?"

"What about individual phone calls and emails; did the consultant get back to you quickly and were they willing to spend the time answering your questions and concerns?"

Speaking from a purely fiscal perspective, a successful consultation should result in the Charity being pleased to pay for what it received. If you are over the age of twenty-one, you know the frustration of paying little and getting even less. This is especially true with governance restructuring. At the best of times the process itself can be draining, so to go down this road and not arrive at your intended destination is not only very frustrating but very counterproductive. You want to avoid leaving a legacy with the Board of "Been there. Done that. Never again." Before you begin, be absolutely clear where you want to be when you arrive at your destination.

Summary

We have seen the importance of engaging someone from the outside to coach a Board through the process of governance restructuring. We have looked at what that process should look like and how long it should take. We have addressed the issue of whether the Board should engage a consultant by the hour or with a flat fee for the entire process. Finally we looked at the importance of getting a consultant who is competent, experienced and connects well with your particular Charity.

> A successful consultation should result in the Charity being pleased to pay for what it received.

In Conclusion

I trust this book has helped you articulate the right questions to be asked about Charity governance. Along with that I trust that you have been provided with some good answers as I have pointed you in the direction of finding more detailed answers to your questions.

Everyone Deserves Good Governance

Every Charity wants to know that because it exists there is an identifiable group of people who are better off. Hungry people are fed, homeless people have a place to live, the vulnerable feel valued, the needy have received some provisions, and those who were without a church home now have a likeminded community of people. Good governance is a benefit to Boards, Leaders and Members. But in the end, good governance ultimately benefits those for whom the Charity exists.

The word "Charity" implies that people will give with no expectation of any material return. Because you have read this book I assume you are one of those individuals. My passion is to specifically help people like you who are sacrificing their time to get the best possible return on the time they are investing.

Because of the time you spend at your next Board meeting, someone needs to be better off. It is my desire that this book will blow wind in the sails of your leadership so you can better serve and someone will be better off.

About the Author

Ted Hull is the President of *Ted Hull Consulting*. He has been involved with churches and para-church organizations for over twenty-five years, serving in executive positions and as a consultant. Ted has a passion to serve churches and charities by facilitating the process of good governance through coaching Boards and Leaders in the course of change.

Ted lives in Winnipeg, Manitoba, with his wife Lorna. He has two children and four grandchildren.

Ted Hull Consulting

So you can better serve

272-3336 Portage Avenue

Winnipeg Manitoba R3K 2H9

204.896.6740

info@tedhullconsulting.com

tedhullconsulting.com

Notes

[i] Carver, John. *Boards that Make a Difference*. 3rd ed. San Francisco: Jossey-Bass, 2006. Print.

[ii] Carver, John and Miriam Carver. *Reinventing Your Board*. Rev. ed. San Francisco: Jossey-Bass, 2006. Print.

[iii] Oliver, Caroline. *Getting Started with Policy Governance*. San Francisco: Jossey-Bass, 2009. Print.

[iv] Douma, Teresa A. *2010 Charities Handbook*. Elmira, Ont.: Canadian Council of Christian Charities, 2010. Print.

[v] Brown, Jim. *The Imperfect Board Member*. San Francisco: Jossey-Bass, 2006. Print.

[vi] Kranendonk, Dick L. *Serving as a Board Member: Protecting Yourself from Legal Liability While Serving Charities*. Rev. ed. Belleville, Ont.: Essence Publishing, 2002. Print.

[vii] Getz, Gene A. *Elders and Leaders: God's Plan for Leading the Church*. Chicago: Moody Publishers, 2003. Print.

viii   Malphurs, Aubrey. *Ministry Nuts and Bolts: What They Don't Teach Pastors in Seminary.* Grand Rapids: Kregel Publications, 1997. Print.

ix   Ghomeshi, Jila. *Grammar Matters.* Winnipeg, Man.: Arbeiter Ring Publishing, 2010. Print.

x   Canadian Volunteerism Institute. *The Canadian Code for Volunteer Involvement.* www.volunteer.ca/files/CodeEng-June2006.pdf Web.